PARANORMAL KENTUCKY

PARANORMAL KENTUCKY

An Uncommon Wealth of Close Encounters with Aliens, Ghosts, and Cryptids

MARIE MITCHELL

&

MASON SMITH

UNIVERSITY PRESS OF KENTUCKY

A note to the reader: This volume contains references to historical instances of sexual assault, racially motivated violence and oppression, and other sensitive topics. Discretion is advised.

Scholarly publisher for the Commonwealth, serving Bellarmine University, Berea College, Centre College of Kentucky, Eastern Kentucky University, The Filson Historical Society, Georgetown College, Kentucky Historical Society, Kentucky State University, Morehead State University, Murray State University, Northern Kentucky University, Spalding University, Transylvania University, University of Kentucky, University of Louisville, University of Pikeville, and Western Kentucky University.

Editorial and Sales Offices: The University Press of Kentucky
663 South Limestone, Lexington, Kentucky 40508-4008
www.kentuckypress.com

Cataloging-in-Publication data is available from the Library of Congress.

ISBN 978-1-9859-0313-5 (hardcover : alk. paper)
ISBN 978-1-9859-0314-2 (paperback : alk. paper)
ISBN 978-1-9859-0315-9 (epub)
ISBN 978-1-9859-0317-3 (pdf)

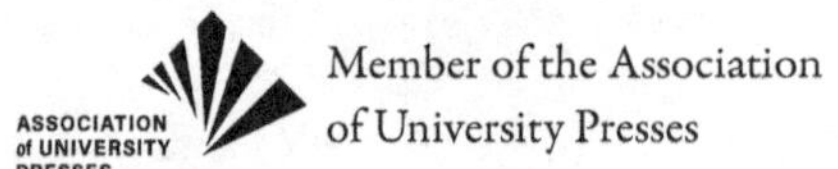

Member of the Association
of University Presses

To our children, Mitchell, Marlowe, Ruby Margaret, and Ingrid, who were raised on paranormal stories and still turned out (mostly) normal. Thanks for humoring us all these years.

CONTENTS

HAUNTED HISTORIC HOMES AND PLACES

OTHER MONSTERS

INTRODUCTION

Ghost Hunting in Kentucky

We wanted to start this book with a crash of thunder, a crescendo of ominous music, and a ghostly whisper to telegraph that we had arrived at Waverly Hills Sanitorium, one of the most haunted locations in Kentucky, on "a dark and stormy night." What better phrase than Edward Bulwer-Lytton's to open a book about paranormal investigations? But that would be both a cliché and inaccurate. Also, it's hard to produce sound effects in a book.

We actually arrived at Waverly Hills on a mild evening in late September 2023 without even a full moon to provide a chilling effect. But judging from the outward appearance of this former tuberculosis hospital in Louisville, you'd think Dr. Frankenstein was upstairs tinkering with his monster. The building looks like it could be teeming with ghosts, ghouls, and elemental spirits—or at least four-legged vermin of one kind or another. Yet we walked up the drive unmolested to reach the back entrance of the sanitorium. The dilapidated building stands on a steep hill only a mile or so from Dixie Highway (US 60) near Pleasure Ridge Park, west of Shively. We couldn't hear the highway traffic from the hilltop. In fact, we couldn't hear much of anything. We were in urban Jefferson County, not far from the lights and noise of downtown Louisville, but the woods surrounding the massive, creepy-looking building were silent.

The structure in front of us—which had fallen into disrepair after being abandoned decades ago—has been investigated countless times by private paranormal investigators and TV crews looking for a quick Halloween feature story. They have found a smorgasbord of shadows, sounds, scurrying animals, echoes, and dripping water—not to mention the pops, cracks, sighs, and groans emitted by old buildings due to changes in temperature and wind pressure. Such groups have also captured what they claim are entities flitting about the place. Maybe that's because a haunted house is what they hoped to find, or perhaps the place really is inhabited by spirits. Who knows?

In 2015 the Waverly Hills Historical Society signed a ninety-nine-year lease and now arranges ghost tours and other events at the venue. After showing our tickets, we entered a dimly lit waiting room—formerly the sanitorium's dining area—and joined nearly a hundred other ghost-hunter wannabes awaiting our respective tour guides. Thankfully, we were wearing jackets, as the gaping windows facing south had never been glassed in, the idea being to give the tuberculosis patients the maximum amount of fresh air and sunshine—a common treatment for this often deadly lung disease, along with commonsense practices such as resting and eating a healthy diet. Only in extreme cases did patients undergo surgery to remove ribs to ease their breathing.

Before the invention of antibiotics, many TB patients faced a slow, painful death. Based on death certificate evidence, paranormal researcher Troy Taylor estimates that as many as six thousand patients died at Waverly Hills from 1910 to 1961.[1] Some of them already had advanced cases of TB before they arrived, as the "white plague" was rapidly spreading across Jefferson County. These might be the lost souls who supposedly walk the dark and silent wards today. However, it's important to note that some patients left the facility cured, and those who didn't at least enjoyed regular meals, movie nights, and art classes they couldn't have afforded otherwise.

Prior to our eight o'clock tour, we were all asked to sign legal waivers in case of injury (or heart attacks from climbing five flights of stairs). The biggest danger we faced was the deep, eerie darkness—the very *darkest* dark one can imagine, like being in a cave—which gave the tour a spooky vibe. This darkness was scarier than any potential spirits we might encounter while feeling our way along the pitch-black corridors, illuminated only by the flashlight our guide carried. We shuffled up and down bare concrete stairs and through dark hallways calling out for the ghostly boy named Timmy, who liked to play with a yellow ball. We begged shadow people to materialize and visited the room on the top floor where a despondent nurse, pregnant and unmarried, allegedly hanged herself.

At one point, a brave young man celebrating his birthday volunteered to walk down a lonely corridor to see if he could startle any "shadow people" out into the open. We could see only his dim outline as he reported, "I'm not sure, but I might see something moving down at the end of the hall." All we could see was a void. A herd of shadow people could have stampeded past us, and we wouldn't have known it. A ghostly glow would have been a welcome sight in those gloomy hallways.

We didn't see any ghosts, but we were thrilled to see firsthand the infamous body chute, a long tunnel used to bring provisions up to the patients and discreetly transport the dead out of the hospital rather than parade them past the occupied rooms and upset the living residents. Our guide shared the experience of seeing a pair of red eyes looking up at her and her friends from the bottom of the body chute and then start moving up the tunnel toward them. Petrified, they realized the red eyes—and whatever they were attached to—had started to pick up speed and were just moments away from them. The group set some speed records themselves that night as they outran the spooky entity—or maybe a raccoon. Under such circumstances, running certainly makes sense to us. That's why we never question why a paranormal witness would flee from a spirit, a bigfoot, or a monster. And that's why we always wear sensible shoes during our investigations.

At the end of the tour, our guide encouraged us to return for an overnight investigation, saying, "You never know what you might see in the early morning hours." We politely declined the invitation, since spending the night in a cold, dark, drafty, dilapidated, and potentially haunted building with troubled spirits, wild critters, and creepy-crawlies isn't our idea of fun.

Our visit to Waverly Hills Sanitorium is one of the many trips we've made to sites of ghostly hauntings, cryptid encounters, and UFO incidents across Kentucky while doing research for this book. We wanted to see for ourselves the places where paranormal events were reported and interview the witnesses to help us explain, in the most unbiased way possible, what they experienced. We couldn't investigate every paranormal occurrence in Kentucky, so we chose the most intriguing ones. Our travels took us to haunted historic homes such as White Hall, abolitionist Cassius Clay's mansion near our own home in Richmond. We took a number of ghost walks across the state, including one in Bardstown with paranormal investigator Patti Starr. We felt the cool spray from Cumberland Falls, where a bride apparently fell to her death and continues to relive the moment, and we marched across Civil War battlefields seeking the spirits of soldiers who never returned home. We were drawn to the Mothman legend, searched for Bigfoot vicariously through other hunters combing the Daniel Boone National Forest, and were on the lookout for a man-wolf at Land Between the Lakes. We even beamed over to several places where UFOs have been well documented—and, to our surprise (and delight), we located an actual spaceship in a western Kentucky park.

Herry the Herrington Lake Monster eluded us, as did Louisville's Demon Leaper and Goatman. We were unable to sit for a séance with former First

Lady Mary Todd Lincoln, and we couldn't visit the off-limits grave of Leah Smock, the only alleged witch who was burned alive in Kentucky, but we can still tell their stories through diligent research.

We promise that this book is much more than a collection of random stories. As retired journalists, that's not how we operate. Mason worked in the newspaper business before earning his PhD and spending the last part of his career teaching English composition at Eastern Kentucky University. Marie spent twenty-four years as WEKU's public radio news director before finishing her career teaching communications at EKU. We also give talks about Kentucky's paranormal activity through the Kentucky Humanities Council's Speakers Bureau. So, our approach to these investigations is colored by our journalistic backgrounds. We are neither true believers nor skeptics. We are merely observers who listen carefully and never assume that a witness is mistaken, lying, or foolish for disclosing whatever "high strangeness" they experienced while going about their normal activities. We present the facts, offer several interpretations, and draw some conclusions. We also provide historical background and context for these reports of unusual occurrences. For example, there's a brief discussion of World War II before we delve into cases of UFOs appearing in Kentucky skies in 1947. And we cover Mothman's appearance in West Virginia in 1967 before we discuss his reported sighting in Kentucky much later. However, we don't claim to have all the answers. Even with our extensive research and interviews, we can't always provide a logical explanation for everything that's happened.

Throughout this book, we've been careful when using the terms *myth*, *legend*, and *tale*. Although in casual conversation we might use these words interchangeably, scholars make important distinctions. For example, folklorists refer to a *myth* as a story told as true, especially one that contains spiritual teachings about gods or demigods. By contrast, a *legend* is understood to be a historical narrative, but one that may have been exaggerated or fictionalized somewhat. Finally, a *tale* is a story told as entertainment and is assumed to be fiction.

In the chapters about Kentucky UFOs, we use the term *unidentified flying objects*, which is what US Air Force Captain Edward J. Ruppelt of Project Blue Book called them in the 1950s. However, NASA and the US and Royal Air Forces now prefer *unidentified anomalous phenomena*, or UAP. But whatever they're called, the question remains: are they swamp gas, weather balloons, the planet Venus, or something else? We have our theories, but they could be revised if new evidence arises. As one of Mason's former professors used to say, “That question merits further research.” Following the UFO section are chapters devoted to ghosts, haunted places, and various monsters.

So, whether you’re reading this book on a warm, sunny day or “a dark and stormy night,” grab your tinfoil hat, lace up your running shoes for a quick escape from strange noises, and keep a flashlight handy (just in case) while you embark on this spine-tingling journey with us.

KENTUCKIANS BATTLE WARTIME FEAR

On a chilly night during the early days of World War II, Frankfort police got calls from several witnesses who reported seeing a periscope—presumably from an enemy U-boat—silently rising and retracting in the dark waters of the Kentucky River. The police immediately notified the US Army, and patrols were ordered to keep an eye on the river just in case a Nazi submarine surfaced and carried out a sneak attack in the heart of the Bluegrass.

Does this scenario sound preposterous? Perhaps it does to us today. And even back then, the state's newspapers never reported the alleged Frankfort U-boat sighting, so the entire story may be false—just an elaborate joke by the source: the father of one of Mason's college buddies. But if you're a conspiracy theorist, you might suspect that this is yet another event suppressed by the government to prevent wartime panic.

Of course, no U-boat was ever found, and Kentuckians were never directly threatened by the Germans on local waterways. At the time, technology allowed submarines to remain submerged for only a few hours at a time, so if a Nazi submarine had actually wanted to shell Frankfort, much of its trip from the open ocean to Kentucky would have been on the surface, for all to see. To reach Frankfort, an enemy ship would have had to pass, undetected, through all the locks along the Mississippi, Ohio, and Kentucky Rivers. In fact, destroying those locks would have better served the Nazis than attacking Kentucky's capital city.

One might wonder how people could be so gullible as to believe such a tale, but in the winter of 1942, fear gripped the nation. Pearl Harbor had just been attacked. Real U-boats were sinking Allied ships by the hundreds. The Japanese were rolling across the Pacific. Frankfort residents had every reason to be scared, but in more rational times, they might have acknowledged that a German U-boat surfacing in the Kentucky River was implausible.

Regardless of whether the reports were true or false, authorities would have had every reason to suppress this story. Past experience proved that wartime panic can be deadly. For example, in the wee hours of February 25, 1942, a weather balloon released by military authorities near Los Angeles set off air-raid sirens across the city. In response, thousands of antiaircraft shells were fired into the night sky.[1] The famous "Battle of Los Angeles" resulted in five deaths: three caused by auto accidents and two by heart attacks. The car collisions occurred because the streetlights and stoplights had been turned off during the air raid. In addition, falling shrapnel injured a number of city residents. But no wreckage from Japanese (or space alien) aircraft ever surfaced, despite the heavy antiaircraft fire. In fact, coastal-defense gunners apparently failed to hit the weather balloon, which was reportedly drifting out to sea about an hour after the barrage started. The lesson is clear: fearful people see danger everywhere.

And we remain fearful today. In the Age of Anxiety, it's hard to recapture the sense of safety that American and British citizens enjoyed before the war. With their nations protected by vast oceans and patrolled by fleets of massive battleships, they believed that nothing could seriously threaten the United States or the United Kingdom. By 1942, however, everyone realized how terribly wrong they'd been, given the German air attacks on London in 1940 and the Japanese bombing of Pearl Harbor in 1941.

As the war progressed, the power and scale of Allied air resources grew at a mind-boggling rate. Mason's father, Lieutenant Charles W. Smith, was stationed in England in June 1944 just before D-Day. He was awakened on the night of June 5 by the roar of warplanes taking off and flying over the English Channel toward occupied France. After that first surge came another and another. Lieutenant Smith witnessed American B-17s and B-24s, plus platoons of fighter planes, American P-51s and P-38s, all headed for France. Additional waves of Douglass C-47 transport planes were right behind them. As the US warplanes rumbled toward the horizon, more planes followed in formation: British Lancaster and Blenheim bombers alongside Spitfires, Hurricanes, and Mosquitoes. A steady stream of squadrons roared above him. Not dozens or hundreds but thousands of warplanes raced toward their target—Normandy. "It never stopped," Smith said of the missions that continued throughout the night and all the next day, June 6, the date of the Allied invasion of Normandy.

By the time World War II ended in September 1945, Americans had developed an intense fear of attack from above, a vast and secret system of civilian and military intelligence gathering, and a massive program of top-secret weapons development geared to counter the Soviet threat. Coincidentally, shortly afterward, in June and July 1947, Americans started to report seeing flying saucers. The Thomas Mantell UFO incident, discussed in the next chapter, occurred near Louisville in January 1948. Interestingly, in a time of increased anxiety about air attacks, people started to see strange things in the air.

UFO researcher Stanton Friedman argued passionately that flying saucers came from extraterrestrial sources, and he believed that the appearance of UFOs was directly related to the war. For decades, Friedman claimed that aliens showed up after World War II because humans had developed atomic bombs and heavy-lift rockets with the ability to drop those bombs on some other country's doorstep—or, perhaps, on some other planet's doorstep. As Friedman put it, aliens now saw humans as "the new kids on the block who liked to play with some very dangerous toys."[2] It should come as no surprise, Friedman argued, that extraterrestrials would be curious about us. And they would be crazy not to zip over and check on us whenever they were in the neighborhood.

Even during the war, Allied and Axis pilots and flight crews had reported "foo fighters," balls of light that seemed to follow the warplanes on their missions. In fact, the origin of these mysterious lights has never been established. Planetary scientist Carl Sagan argued in *The Demon-Haunted World* that many—and perhaps most—UFO reports might be the result of new weapons developed during World War II and the Cold War. After all, there *were* strange aircraft in the skies—new rockets, missiles, jets, and even hybrid craft such as the X-15—flying where "no one had gone before," to paraphrase *Star Trek*.[3] And, of course, the United States was (and still is) developing stealth aircraft and who knows what else at restricted locations such as the famous Area 51 near Groom Lake, Nevada. Although it is still highly classified, the base is apparently operated by the US Air Force and Lockheed's Skunk Works Research and Development Division. It is interesting to note how often the military seems to be present at or near these UFO events, which leads to a discussion of government cover-ups.

This chapter opened with a threat from beneath the waves, so in keeping with that theme, let's consider one of the most famous water monsters: Nessie, a creature said to resemble a ten- to fifteen-foot-long plesiosaurus that supposedly inhabits Loch Ness in Scotland, a lake a fraction of the size of Kentucky Lake. Although many of the famous photos of Nessie have been debunked as hoaxes, some early reports remain unexplained to this day. So what exactly were people seeing in the dark waters of Loch Ness during the interwar years?

One possibility is a top-secret weapons platform being tested by the Royal Navy. In the late stages of World War I, the British developed and built more than a dozen K-boats, which were steam-powered submarines, or basically submersible destroyers. As it turned out, K-boats were a terrible idea. Of the eighteen K-class submarines built, six sank due to faulty design or accidents, and several more were almost lost due to poor engineering and handling difficulties. The Royal Navy ran the K-boats' clandestine sea trials in the lochs of Scotland, and the program remained secret for years, not only because the Admiralty wanted to protect a massive weapons system from the Germans but also because it was a disaster that wasted millions of pounds and cost hundreds of British lives—a debacle the bureaucrats needed to hide from Parliament and the British people. According to researcher Don Everitt: "All but one of the K disasters escaped public attention because of wartime censorship. The courts of inquiry and courts martial were held in secret. After the armistice, the Admiralty released no more information about them than the bare statistics it was obliged to give to the *Official Return of Navy Losses*. In forty years only a few brief accounts, fragmentary and often largely hearsay, have appeared in naval literature, technical journals and obituary columns."[4]

How interesting that people reported seeing a large, dark mass in Loch Ness at the same time the military was developing a new weapons program.

As we know, official secrets are not just a British problem. US presidents have hidden facts that were likely well known to the Russians, the Chinese, and other nations that might not have Americans' best interests at heart. Think of the Watergate break-in and cover-up of the 1970s, the Iran-Contra scandal of the 1980s, or, more recently, the nefarious Ukraine quid pro quo case that got Donald Trump impeached for the first time in 2019. Presidents attempt to keep secrets from Congress and the American people, arguing executive privilege and national security. But sometimes "official secrets" protect only the officials themselves. And perhaps disclosing those secrets to the public would go a long way toward alleviating some of the paranormal panic revealed in the following chapters.

"I'M CLOSING ON IT"

War Hero Dies Chasing a UFO

Kentucky's first and perhaps most famous UFO incident occurred on January 7, 1948, when Captain Thomas Mantell, a Kentucky Air National Guard pilot, died while chasing an unusual object spotted in the air near Madisonville. During World War II, the twenty-five-year-old Mantell had been awarded the Distinguished Flying Cross for heroism while completing a mission under heavy antiaircraft fire. His war record also included flying in the D-Day air armada. Mantell was praised for being able to think fast and act quickly.

On this fateful day, Mantell, the flight leader, and three other pilots in P-51 (later renamed F-51) Mustangs were taking part in a routine flight from Marietta, Georgia. At around 2:45 p.m., officials at Godman Air Force Base at Fort Knox radioed the pilots and asked them to investigate an unidentified object moving south across central Kentucky. The base commander, Colonel Guy Hix, described the object as white with a red border at the bottom and "about one-fourth the size of the full moon." It was big enough to be seen through binoculars.

One of the four pilots was low on fuel and returned to base shortly afterward. Mantell and the other two, also World War II veterans, continued to search. A Louisville newspaper reported that Lieutenant A. W. Clements spotted the object and observed that it looked like a bright shining star. According to the article, the other pilot, Lieutenant B. A. Hammond, followed Mantell and Clements until they reached twenty thousand feet, at which point he started feeling "woozy" and was "seeing double." He signaled his distress to Clements.[1] Although Clements had an oxygen mask, the tanks had not been charged for the short flight to Fort Knox. For their own safety, the two pilots returned to base.

Meanwhile, Mantell radioed that he had sighted the UFO and was going to try to catch up to it.[2] Mantell's last radio contact came at 3:15 p.m., when he indicated that the object was matching his speed and climbing well past twenty thousand feet. Mantell still hoped to get a closer look but reported that he would abandon the chase if the object got too far ahead to intercept.

Minutes later, Mantell's plane crashed near a farm in Franklin in Simpson County, close to the Tennessee border. (Strangely enough, Mantell was born in Franklin, not far from where his plane crashed. What are the odds?) Pieces of the plane were strewn over a wide area; the fuel tank was located about a half mile away from the main wreckage, and the tail section was discovered a quarter mile away. Mantell's body was found, intact, still belted in his seat in the cockpit. His watch had stopped at 3:18 p.m., presumably the moment of the crash.[3]

Since the Mantell incident is among the earliest and most dramatic UFO encounters, it generated national headlines. According to Captain Edward J. Ruppelt, one of the first directors of Project Blue Book, the air force's official UFO investigative office, late editions of the January 7, 1948, *Louisville Courier-Journal* contained this headline: "F-51 and Capt. Mantell Destroyed Chasing Flying Saucer."[4] However, we couldn't locate the headline or the story in newspaper archives. The January 8 edition of the *Courier-Journal* described the crash but made no mention of flying saucers. Nevertheless, the story of Mantell's death was carried on the national news wires, and many of the headlines were sensational. Suddenly aliens weren't just something to speculate about at the barbershop. People now wondered whether the earth was being threatened by extraterrestrial beings.

UFO researcher Donald Keyhoe opened his 1950 book, *The Flying Saucers Are Real*, with the Mantell incident, capturing the mood of the air force officers crowded into the tower at Godman Field at 2:45 p.m.:

> The first alarm had come from Fort Knox, where Army M.P.s had relayed a state police warning. A huge gleaming object had been seen in the sky, moving toward Godman Field. Hundreds of startled people had seen it at Madisonville, ninety miles away.
>
> Thirty minutes later, it had zoomed up over the base. Colonel Guy Hix glanced around at the rest of the men in the tower. They all had a dazed look. Every man there had seen the thing, as it barreled south of the field. Even through the thin clouds, its intermittent red glow had

> hinted at some mysterious source of power. Something outside their understanding.
>
> "I've sighted the thing!" he [Mantell] said. "It looks metallic—and it's tremendous in size!"
>
> The C.O., Hix, and Woods stared at each other. No one spoke. "The thing's starting to climb," Mantell said swiftly. "It's at twelve o'clock high, making half my speed. I'll try to close in."
>
> At 3:08, Mantell's wingman called in. Both he and the other pilot had seen the weird object. But Mantell had outclimbed them and was lost in the clouds.
>
> Then at 3:15, Mantell made a hasty contact.
>
> "It's still above me, making my speed or better. I'm going up to twenty thousand feet. If I'm no closer, I'll abandon chase."
>
> It was his last report.[5]

Keyhoe's account was originally published in *True*, a men's magazine featuring stories on sports, lifestyle, and the outdoors. Most (but not all) of the witnesses agreed that the object was shiny and silverish and had what might have been lights at the top and bottom. And despite Keyhoe's contention that the object "zoomed up over the base" and "barreled south of the field," the majority said it hung almost stationary in the sky and then drifted slowly to the south and west.

When Keyhoe later expanded his sensational article into a book, it became a best seller. Its popularity could be attributed to his argument that air force officials knew more about UFOs than they were telling the public, making him one of the first UFO researchers to suggest a UFO cover-up conspiracy.

No recording exists of the actual radio communications between Mantell and the base, so we must rely on the memories of the men in the tower that winter afternoon.[6] For example, according to Ruppelt, everyone in the tower heard Mantell say, "I'm going to 20,000 feet." However, that would be bizarre. As Ruppelt notes, "Every pilot and crewman has it pounded into him, 'Do not, under any circumstances, go above 15,000 feet without oxygen.'"[7] Mantell's World War II–era P-51 was not equipped with oxygen for the short hop from Marietta. So why would a trained pilot disobey this most basic of all flight rules, especially one that would put him in grave danger?

After Mantell's untimely death, rumors spread about the cause of the crash. There was speculation that the plane had been downed by a Soviet missile or struck by hostile aliens or that it had disintegrated in the air; there were also stories that the wreckage was radioactive. In addition, rumor had it that Mantell's body was riddled with bullets or missing entirely. Ruppelt discounts such conjecture. He notes that, according to the accident report, the plane's wreckage was not shot up, burned, or radioactive; nor did the plane blow up. Witnesses on the ground said the plane descended in a tight spiral, losing its wings and perhaps its tail assembly as it fell. It struck the ground and was ripped apart by the impact.

Air force investigators concluded that Mantell had apparently flown above the oxygen ceiling and lost consciousness, causing his plane to go into a tight stall. He died on impact, *not* in a dogfight with space aliens.

UFO researcher Richard Dolan wrote this about the Mantell incident: "He had climbed too high without oxygen, and certainly passed out. What he chased remains unclear to this day. Project Sign initially thought he had misidentified Venus, which was in the general direction he was going, until it was realized there was too much daylight for Venus to have been visible. They then changed their solution to 'Unknown.' Some years later, astronomer J. Allen Hynek suggested Mantell might have chased one of the Navy's classified Project Skyhook balloons."[8]

Project Sign was the US Air Force's first UFO investigative office, created in 1948. It was replaced by Project Grudge in 1949 and Project Blue Book in 1950, which continued until 1969. Blue Book's cancellation supposedly ended the government's interest in flying saucers. However, the *New York Times* reported in 2017 that the air force was still studying UFOs with the Advanced Aerospace Threat Identified Program (AATIP).

After reviewing the files related to the incident and reinvestigating parts of it years later, Ruppelt wrote:

> About the only theory left to check was that the object might have been one of the Navy's big, 100-foot-diameter "Skyhook" balloons. I rechecked the descriptions of the UFO made by the people in the tower. The first man to sight the object called it a parachute, others said ice cream cone, round, etc. All of these descriptions fit a balloon. Buried deep in the file were two more references to balloons that I had previously missed. Not long after the object had disappeared from view at Godman AFB, a man from Madisonville, Kentucky, called Flight Service in Dayton. He had seen an object traveling southeast. He had looked at it through a telescope, and it was a balloon. At four forty-five an astronomer living north

of Nashville, Tennessee, called in. He had also seen a UFO, looked at it through a telescope, and it was a balloon.[9]

Project Skyhook was a classified program to study cosmic rays and record meteorological observations at very high altitudes. It was operated by the US Navy's Office of Naval Research, and the project's scientists may have launched a research balloon on January 7, 1948, from Clinton County Air Force Base in southern Ohio. Ruppelt, however, was unable to confirm a balloon launch on that date because of damaged records. Someone had apparently spilled coffee or cola on the microfilm.[10] But with more than fifteen hundred launches during the program's ten-year lifespan from the mid-1940s through the mid-1950s, Ruppelt believed a balloon launch on that particular date was likely. At 100 feet tall, the Skyhook balloons were designed to reach altitudes of up to 100,000 feet, and according to Ruppelt, the shiny balloons could be seen at 60,000 feet. Brilliantly lit up by the afternoon sun, the Skyhook balloon and its instrument package might have appeared close, but in fact it would have been *miles* above the flight ceiling of Mantell's P-51 Mustang.

So what does this all mean? As the old saying goes, if it looks like a duck, flies like a duck, and quacks like a duck, it's *probably* a duck. Given the available evidence, Mantell was *probably* chasing a large, shiny research balloon rather than an interplanetary visitor. And yet, if observers on the ground could identify the object as a balloon, why couldn't Mantell do so at closer range? Although Mantell didn't have access to a telescope or binoculars in his cockpit, as some of the ground observers did, several of those witnesses, using only their naked eyes, could at least see that the object was balloon shaped.

Another puzzling question is why Mantell would have been intrigued enough to violate one of the primary rules of flight by taking his plane above twenty thousand feet in an attempt to identify the mysterious object. That decision proved fatal. Mantell was a highly trained pilot, but he didn't have much experience flying the new P-51 Mustang. Perhaps the crash was caused by pilot error due to a lack of training at the controls. Still, like a good soldier, Mantell was obeying an order to investigate an unidentified flying object that might have been harmless or might have been a hostile intruder that posed a threat to national security. The question is, what was Mantell *expecting* to find as he flew alone through "the long, delirious, burning blue"?[11]

Ruppelt points out that everyone—including the tower personnel at Godman Field—was fixated on flying saucers at the time. When one's mind is focused on "alien spacecraft," it's hard to make one's eyes see "research balloon."

Perhaps Mantell pushed his limits because he thought he was close to solving the greatest mystery of the twentieth century. Was his obsession fueled by the thought of becoming a hero? Or were his actions more altruistic, based on a desire to protect Americans from a potentially aggressive adversary?

As we wrap up this discussion, there are three important points to remember. First, military secrecy comes into play. Specifically, the Office of Naval Research didn't inform the army that it was launching a research balloon in southern Ohio, and this culture of secrecy could have cost a decorated service member his life. Repeatedly, mysterious UFO sightings are reported in proximity to military operations. For example, the two famous Tic-Tac UFO incidents of the 1990s, in which suspicious objects were recorded on infrared cameras, occurred in areas where military operations were being conducted off the West and East Coasts of the United States. Military involvement is a recurring factor in UFO cases.

Second, when we conclude that the Mantell incident *probably* involved the misidentification of a Project Skyhook balloon, we're trying to be as scientific as possible. Science is not about Truth (note the capital letter) but about probabilities. For example, a scientist might say, "When these conditions prevail, this outcome happens *most of the time*." There is very little certainty in science, only likelihood.

Finally, people sometimes do unpredictable things, even highly trained military officers like Captain Thomas Mantell. Men and women who get caught up in the moment can make poor decisions they would never make under normal circumstances. Mantell may have been as captivated as everyone else with the UFO craze, and in the hope of unraveling this mystery, he might have flown too high for his own safety and died as a result.

The bottom line is that Captain Mantell almost certainly did *not* engage in a dogfight with a flying saucer. Still, the incident has entered American popular culture. Mantell's UFO chase was supposedly the inspiration for the *Star Trek* episode "Tomorrow Is Yesterday," in which the *Enterprise* is transported back to the 1960s and spotted by an air force pilot who gives chase—like Mantell. The fictional pilot is beamed aboard the *Enterprise* and then ultimately returned safely to his own cockpit in one of *Star Trek*'s famous time-travel contradictions.[12] If only that had been possible in real life.

Thomas Mantell Jr. is buried in Zachary Taylor National Cemetery in Louisville. A historical marker outside the Simpson County Tourism Office commemorates his crash near Franklin, Kentucky. The marker, unveiled in late 2001, says, "Much speculation and conjecture has been written about the incident. It is still uncertain what Mantell was pursuing at the time of the crash." Perhaps it should say that he died chasing a Cold War artifact considered too classified to be shared even with another branch of the US military. Although such secrets are often considered necessary for national security, they can cause senseless, avoidable casualties without furthering our understanding of the unknown.

Researcher Kevin D. Randle ends his discussion of the Mantell incident with this observation: "But a mystery remains. What did Mantell see? What made an experienced pilot continue to an altitude he knew would kill quickly? It must have been something so important that Mantell felt he had to take the risk. We may never know what he saw, but it is almost certain that it wasn't a balloon or Venus. He was too experienced to be killed trying to fly to Venus."[13] But the type of balloon Randle refers to is the standard NOAA weather balloon, not the new high-altitude Skyhook research vehicle with a helium-filled plastic envelope that would have expanded to an egg shape spanning up to thirty meters in diameter. It would have glittered in the winter afternoon sun like polished metal. And it would have appeared to be flying without wings, engines, or rudders. No wonder Captain Mantell thought he was chasing an alien craft and risked his life to determine whether it was a threat to the country he served.

ALIEN ATTACK

Family Shoots at "Little Men" from UFO

In 1955 newspapers across the country carried front-page headlines such as "Kentucky Family Describes Mysterious Little Men Who Visited Their Farm in Space Ship," "Night of the 'Little Green Men,'" and "Local Residents Left Gog-Eyed over Flying Saucer Reports." They refer to a disturbing encounter between a western Kentucky farm family and up to a dozen glowing, three-foot-tall "little men" who terrorized them throughout the night of August 21, 1955. Two of the adults engaged in a one-sided gun battle against the intruders, who peeked in the windows and harassed the family for hours. Among the most well documented UFO cases, it's listed as one of the "classics" by Edward Ruppelt, the first director of Project Blue Book.[1]

This frightening incident occurred near Hopkinsville, outside the tiny town of Kelly with a population of 150—mainly farmers—plus a gas station and a few small churches.[2] The overnight ordeal that shook eight adults and three children inspired countless movies, including *E.T. the Extra-Terrestrial* in 1982, and episodes of several TV shows, such as *The Twilight Zone* and *The X-Files*. Even a Pokémon, Sableye, is based on the creatures who dropped by uninvited and overstayed their earthly visit.

One imaginative reporter called the aliens "Little Green Men," which caught on despite eyewitnesses describing them as being silver-skinned, wearing silver suits, or having bodies that were nickel-plated or like aluminum foil. Apparently, "green" was already part of our collective imagination where aliens were concerned. The Hopkinsville–Christian County Convention and Visitors Bureau refers to Rudyard Kipling's 1906 children's book *Puck of Pook's Hill*, in which the little green men are actually humans tattooed green. Edgar Rice Burroughs's 1912 novel *A Princess on Mars* depicts Martians as green. And in 1934, twenty-fifth-century comic book hero Buck Rogers battled green alien monsters. By 1961, "little green men" were referenced in the *Oxford English Dictionary* as "mysterious beings, alleged to have been seen emerging from flying saucers." The "uninvited, unexpected, and unearthly" visitors mentioned in the *Encyclopedia of Monsters* were also referred to as gremlins, space men, Mars men, flying tubmen, goblins, and hobgoblins—take your pick.[3]

Whoever they were, and whatever their color, their sudden appearance caused a commotion. Here's what happened that night in 1955, based on official reports, newspaper and magazine articles, books, and other sources we consulted:

The family, including twenty-five-year-old Lucky Sutton and his fifty-year-old mother, Glennie Lankford, plus some guests had spent the day rabbit hunting, visiting relatives, or attending Sunday services at the nearby Kelly Holiness Church. They gathered at the farmhouse for supper at around 6:30 p.m. After the meal, while the women readied the children for bed, the men started a card game. Even with the doors and windows open, it was hot inside the house, which had electricity but no air-conditioning and no indoor plumbing or running water. Between hands, twenty-one-year-old Billy Ray Taylor, a family friend, went outside to cool off. He rushed back into the house, insisting that he'd seen bright blinking lights from a flying saucer that looked "round and metallic" and had streaks trailing behind it "like the colors of the rainbow." Billy Ray swore that it landed behind some trees in a nearby cornfield.[4] According to Lucky's daughter, Geraldine Sutton Stith, no one believed Billy Ray at first, since he was known to be a prankster. However, everyone grew concerned when the family's hound dog, Old Blue, began frantically barking and Billy Ray and Lucky found him cowering under the house, "tail tucked between its legs," obviously spooked by something.[5]

The mystery quickly intensified when the men noticed a luminescent little man approaching the house from the field where Billy Ray said the UFO had landed. All the adult witnesses described the creature as short with large, round, glowing eyes; long arms; claws or talons on his hands; a muscular torso but thin, spindly, stick-like legs; webbed feet; a bald head; a cone-like nose with a ball on the end; no neck; and a small slit for a mouth. His ears were large, like an elephant's, and they flapped or wobbled when the creature moved. Also, the intruder didn't walk. He either hopped, floated, or skimmed above the ground or used his long arms to propel himself, like a chimpanzee. Everyone referred to the alien as "he," although there was no way to tell its gender.

By all accounts, the creature had his hands raised in a friendly gesture indicating that he came in peace. He carried no weapon, made no movements that appeared hostile, and did not speak or make any sound. If the creature was extraterrestrial, perhaps he was simply lost and needed directions. Maybe he was searching for somewhere to refuel for the long journey home. Or perhaps he just wanted to introduce himself—and later his buddies. Yet the family felt threatened by the creature's startling arrival and bizarre behavior, so Billy Ray and Lucky reached for their guns: a double-barreled shotgun and a .22-caliber pistol. Lucky guarded the front door, Billy Ray positioned himself at the back door, and the women hid the sleepy children under a bed. Although the intruders never tried to get inside, they apparently looked in the windows, lurked around the house, and even climbed up on the roof.

The *Washington Post* and *Times-Herald* reported on August 22, 1955, that the creatures kept coming closer even after the men fired warning shots into the air. So the next shot was aimed directly at the aliens at close range, about twenty feet. Over the next twenty minutes, the men fired fifty rounds, causing considerable damage to the house but apparently not injuring the trespassers. In fact, the bullets seemed to ricochet off them and made a "clanging" sound, as if striking metal. If the impact stunned the aliens, the spry fellows quickly recovered, did a backflip, fled into the nearby woods, and hid in the trees.

The Suttons didn't have a phone, so they couldn't call for help. The gunfire continued off and on for the next few hours. Still, the aliens didn't retaliate. One on the roof grabbed Billy Ray's hair with its clawed hands, but that seemed more like petting a dog than trying to harm him. While hunkered down, the family noticed that the aliens didn't like the light—it seemed to hurt their eyes. And loud talking or yelling appeared to hurt their ears.

During the standoff, Glennie tried to get some sleep but woke up screaming when she spotted one of the little men staring into her bedroom window. Lucky and Billy Ray rushed to her aid and opened fire—shooting out part of the window screen.

Eventually the family ran low on ammunition, so at around 11:00 p.m., during an eerie silence, the "physically and emotionally drained" adults grabbed the hysterical children, dashed to their two trucks, and raced eight miles to the Hopkinsville police station. The panicked people all started talking at once, until the desk sergeant calmed them down. "We need help," one man pleaded. "We've been fighting little men all night," Glennie added.[6]

The family explained their predicament and expressed their fear that the aliens would return. Police Chief Russell Greenwell, who had arrived to handle the curious emergency, was convinced that their story was sincere; everyone seemed to be sober, and all eleven had genuinely been unnerved by something.

Greenwell called for reinforcements, and twenty officers responded. Hopkinsville police, Christian County sheriff's deputies, Kentucky State Police troopers, and even some military police from nearby Fort Campbell, toting machine guns, rifles, and pistols, sped to the scene at around 12:30 a.m. (The army base stressed that the MPs were acting on their own and not on orders.) The authorities searched for about ninety minutes but found no evidence of a crime scene other than the bullet holes left by the family's gunshots. Missing were blood, bodies, and footprints.

Though there wasn't any definitive proof of a UFO landing in the field, Chief Greenwell found a "strange luminous patch of grass where the creature allegedly fell" from a tree. And one of the witness's relatives, Gail Cook, later insisted that there was "a big, burnt spot out there where nothin' would grow." But the August 7, 2005, edition of the *Tennessean* reported that such a depression could have been a sinkhole, a common occurrence in western Kentucky.[7] Later, the Sutton family insisted that no clues were found because the searchers were using flashlights, and the creatures could only be seen in the dark, when they glowed. That's why the family had been huddled inside the house with the lights off.

After all the officers left at around 2:00 a.m., the family claimed the little men returned. More shots were fired until around 5:15 a.m., when the aliens finally tired of their first contact with the hostile human race and left—not necessarily with a good impression of Kentucky hospitality. Their departure was apparently as spectacular as their entrance, with the spaceship, resembling a bathtub, emitting exhaust that was all the colors of the rainbow.

Unfortunately, the next day brought more invaders—hordes of neighbors, reporters, and other curiosity seekers. Police set up roadblocks to control the crowd. The exhausted family tried to do "normal" things to take their minds off the unsettling night. The men went hunting or ran errands. That left the women and children to put up "No Trespassing" signs to discourage onlookers from walking around the property. When that didn't work, the family tried to charge a fifty-cent admission fee, "one dollar for information, and ten dollars for taking pictures." However, they "never collected one penny."[8] The crowds just kept coming. People even walked right into the house and weren't shy about stealing souvenirs. All those people tramping through the field and around the house would have destroyed any evidence that might have been missed the previous night.

Local reaction to the UFO story was mixed. Some thought it was a hoax and called the Suttons "delusional." According to Geraldine, her father was bitter about the shabby treatment they received and blamed it on the fact that they were poor and not well educated, and some of them were carnival workers. Lucky resented the taunts from people who had no clue about the terrifying ordeal they'd been through.

Several weeks later, Glennie sold the farm, and she and her younger children moved to an apartment complex in Hopkinsville, where they felt safer being around other people. According to Geraldine, her grandmother said the farmhouse didn't feel like home anymore. The house wasn't in the best condition in 1955, and the damage caused by the bullets certainly didn't improve its looks or structural integrity. It was eventually torn down. But a replica spaceship was erected in Kelley Station Park on Old Madisonville Road near where the house once stood. We've seen the impressive human-sized craft ourselves. You can't miss it. The park is also where Little Green Men Days was held for fifteen years until 2020.

Most of the Kelly eyewitnesses have died, and we couldn't find any recorded interviews with them. Adam May, news director of WHOP radio in Hopkinsville, checked his audio archives, "but the recordings for Kelly must not have been kept."[9]

As you can tell, this is a story of ordinary people experiencing extraordinary things. It's unlikely the Suttons staged a giant hoax. No one signed a contract for a book or movie deal. The family was ridiculed by the community and moved away shortly afterward. Lucky's daughter Geraldine told a *Kentucky New Era* reporter in 2002 that her dad wouldn't even talk to her about the alien encounter until he was in his sixties, but he said the memory would stay with him until the day he died. (He passed away in 1995.)[10] And Lucky insisted that they had nothing to gain by making up the story. In her book *Alien Legacy*, Geraldine also discounts the possibility of someone playing a prank on the family. She notes that "most people would take off running after the first gunfire. No one would stay with shotguns going off, risking the chance of getting killed, because that's what would have happened."[11]

Joe Nickell of *Skeptical Inquirer* personally scrutinized the case on its fiftieth anniversary in August 2005. He noted that not all eleven people at the farmhouse actually saw the little men. At least one woman, Billy Ray Taylor's wife, June, refused to look at them, and the children were hiding under a bed. Nickell also points out that Billy Ray, a key witness, revised his original statement several times and elaborated on his initial report, which, frankly, makes the skeptics even more skeptical. In addition, Nickell found it odd that although they were hit by bullets, the little men didn't bleed, fall down, drop dead, or disintegrate into a ball of extraterrestrial goo. Rather, they somersaulted and then ran or hopped away, unaffected by the bullets.[12]

Keep in mind that this incident took place in 1955, which was only a few years into the flying saucer craze. It was a popular, timely topic that was frequently discussed in the media and no doubt in local cafés and barbershops, even in small towns like Kelly, Kentucky. Although they didn't have a TV, we can assume that the Suttons had heard or read about flying saucers, providing them with mental pictures of aliens and UFOs for their imaginations to draw on.

Remember, too, that some of the witnesses had attended a holiness church service that Sunday. What if the emotionally charged service left the family in an overstimulated state, which made them more susceptible to the idea of a visitation from above—in this case, not from heaven but from another star system? It would be interesting to know what text the sermon was based on.

If the family wasn't rattled by a religious message, then skeptics like Nickell argue that they could have been scared by a parliament (flock) of great horned owls rather than visitors from space. Here's how Nickell explains the owl hypothesis: "Echoing descriptions of the Kelly 'little men,' the Great Horned Owl has a height of some 25 inches; very large, staring, yellow eyes; long ear tufts; a large head (set without apparent neck) on its shoulders; a light-gray underside; with talons; and so on. An owl could be on a roof or in a tree and be perceived to 'float' to the ground. As to their behavior, Great Horned Owls are extremely aggressive when defending the nest and their activity typically begins at dusk."[13] The great horned owl matches many of the reported facts of the case, and Kentucky does have breeding populations of these birds. But wouldn't a farm family recognize an owl or at least realize they were dealing with some sort of bird? Owls fly silently, but they need wings to do it. Plus, would owls peep in windows and continue to harass humans who are shooting at them?

Dr. J. Allen Hynek, the scientific adviser for the air force's Project Blue Book, noted, "Under a barrage of gunfire from Kentuckians over a somewhat extended period of time, it is unthinkable that at least one cadaver would not have been found."[14] Hynek is the researcher who created a schema for classifying UFO reports. His system has three categories for distant sightings: lights at night, daylight disks, and radar reports. Plus, there are three categories for close encounters: the first kind is a sighting of some unknown object at close range; the second kind is a sighting that includes some form of physical evidence, such as marks on the ground or scorch marks on trees or grass; and the third kind, like the Kelly-Hopkinsville Incident, involves the sighting of UFO occupants—actual alien contact.

Geraldine Stith believes that others saw lights in the woods that August night but didn't want to risk their reputations by filing a report. She may be right. UFO researcher J. T. Gooch cites an August 22, 1955, *Kentucky New Era* article stating that police Sergeant Frank Dudas and another officer had seen flying saucers the previous summer. And George Barker, writing in the *Nashville Tennessean Magazine* on October 13, 1957, noted that, at the time of the Kelly sighting, several people reported seeing meteors passing overhead "with noise like artillery fire."[15] Artillery fire? That potential military connection provides another explanation of the worrisome encounter: government involvement. It's suspicious that the MPs from Fort Campbell, ten miles away, investigated the Kelly scene—even if they hadn't "officially" been ordered to do so.

In her 2010 book, Leslie Kean mentions a serious fear that gripped US agencies during the Cold War: "In 1938, Orson Welles's famous radio broadcast of *The War of the Worlds* panicked numerous listeners with its all-too-realistic dramatization of an invasion by Martian spaceships, presented as if it were a live, unfolding news report. People actually fled their New Jersey homes—the site of the alleged invasion—and many others were convinced that the Earth was indeed under attack and we all would die."[16] That broadcast incited a real public panic, although Nick Pope, who investigated UFO phenomena for the British government, argues that the media exaggerated the extent of the panic.[17] Still, phone lines in New Jersey were jammed for hours. Highways were blocked. Shots were fired at water towers across the mid-Atlantic states because frightened New Jersey residents mistook the structures for invading Martians.

This reaction got the US government's attention. Based on documents released under the Freedom of Information Act, FBI and CIA officials were apparently worried throughout the early 1950s that the Soviets would stage a fake alien invasion to scare Americans and cover a genuine attack on the United States. These "UFO documents" were internal government memos that were kept from the American public not because they contained evidence of alien contact but because they revealed the government's concern about an attack from a very real but earthly enemy—the Soviet Union.

Indeed, the odd creatures reported at Kelly in 1955 and in a similar incident in Flatwoods, West Virginia, in 1952 seem almost too weird to be *actual* aliens but just weird enough to be a military or CIA experiment designed in the feverish atmosphere of the Cold War. Allen Dulles, CIA director at the time of the incident, has been called the "godfather of dirty tricks." According to author David Talbot, Dulles believed the law—whether American law or international law—did not apply to him. Any number of irresponsible and deadly plots were hatched and carried out during his tenure (1953–1961). For example, Dulles and the CIA reportedly tried to murder Cuban leader Fidel Castro using exploding cigars, and the Bay of Pigs fiasco was also his brainchild. Conducting a frightening "experiment" on American citizens on American soil was exactly the kind of thing Dulles would order if he wanted to know how average people would react to a fake Soviet-sponsored UFO invasion scenario.[18] If the whole point was to expose Americans to a staged "alien invasion" and gauge their reaction, then the up-close and personal approach—including climbing on a roof and peeking in windows—makes sense. It's impossible to say what actual aliens might do if shot at fairly close range, but the reported behavior of the little men in Kelly sounds more like marionettes—artificial targets suspended and dangled in front of the witnesses to get their attention—rather than a living entity, whether extraterrestrial or owl.

Witnesses who saw Kentucky's goblins and West Virginia's Flatwoods monster were terrified, but there was no widespread chaos. The media reported both incidents, and the public, though intrigued, didn't freak out, sending a strong message to the Soviet Union: that a group of Americans faced with an alien invasion didn't faint, surrender, or run screaming into the streets. They hid the kids, loaded their guns, and started shooting.

THE LONG ROAD HOME

Three Women Abducted by Aliens

What started out as a pleasant dinner among friends turned into a shocking and traumatic experience for three Casey County women. After an alcohol-free, spur-of-the-moment celebration of Mona Stafford's thirty-sixth birthday at a favorite restaurant near Lancaster on January 6, 1976, Stafford and her two friends, Louise Smith and Elaine Thomas, headed home to Liberty. The women left at 11:15 on that cold, cloudy night and expected a thirty-five-minute drive. Everything seemed normal as they sped past farmland along Kentucky Highway 78, with Smith at the wheel of her 1967 Chevrolet Nova. However, as the trio departed Stanford, the conversation suddenly stopped when the women spotted an object in the sky that looked like an airplane on fire. It was losing altitude fast, and they watched, horrified, as the aircraft came "hurtling toward the ground," according to Emma Austin's 2021 *Louisville Courier-Journal* article.[1]

However, instead of crashing, the object came to an abrupt halt, hovering directly above Smith's car. UFO researcher Jerome Clark writes: "The witnesses discerned a disc shape with round windows; around each [window], a blinking red light rotated in a counterclockwise direction. A row of yellow lights stretched beneath these. The object was topped with a luminous blue dome. Stafford recalled, 'The dome was blinding, and it reflected on a metallic surface which I'm sure was more than one hundred feet wide.'"[2] Stafford told *Casey County News* reporter Larry Rowell in 2010 that she couldn't take her eyes off the craft. "It was the most scariest and beautiful thing I [had] ever seen."[3]

According to an *Ace Weekly* article by Christopher Kemp, the women thought the blue dome might be a Kentucky State Police officer investigating the mysterious object, but they couldn't wait around to find out. The car suddenly accelerated on its own, even though Smith's foot wasn't on the gas pedal.[4] A frantic Smith tried futilely to stop the Chevy as it raced along the curvy road at eighty-five miles per hour. John Greenewald, writing for theblackvault.com, reported that a terrified Smith shouted, "I can't hold the car on the road."[5] Stafford, sitting in the front seat, tried to help Smith steer, but to no avail. The car began to shimmy and shake, and the frightened women realized that the unknown craft, described as bigger than two houses, was chasing them, matching their perilous speed.

Smith recalled that the car then filled with "a haze-like air, sort of a fog," and all three women reported feeling a "burning sensation so strong that they could not open their eyes."[6] That's when the car was yanked backward toward a pasture with a stone wall entrance, seeming to hit speed bumps along the way. The next thing they knew, they were on the outskirts of Hustonville, eight miles from their initial encounter with the UFO. They were dazed and confused and had no clue how they got there.[7] Also, they had completely lost track of time. When they reached Smith's home, they were shocked to find that it was 1:20 a.m., which meant that it had been two hours since they left the restaurant. Each of the women had "a red mark like a burn on the back of their necks, and they all had burning, irritated eyes."[8] The minute hand on Smith's watch was spinning, and later, after she touched her alarm clock, it stopped working.

The women reluctantly told their story to the police, who showed little interest. But the women's terrifying tale piqued the media's interest and made national headlines, although the women didn't seek or appreciate the publicity.

After their encounter, the women suffered severe headaches, they couldn't sleep, and no matter how much water they drank, they were always thirsty. They lost weight and chain-smoked, fearful that the UFO might return. The three friends couldn't remember if they had simply blacked out or if they had been abducted, probed, and experimented on during the time they lost.[9]

According to Austin's *Courier-Journal* article, Stafford told the *Lexington Leader* in 1977 that she thought about the upsetting encounter every day and was afraid of being abducted again. "It keeps me torn up," she said. "I tried to talk about it to people. They wouldn't listen." Stafford consulted her doctor about the lingering burning sensation around her neck, face, and eyes, and he said it looked like she had been exposed to radiation. Smith experienced similar physical pain. In addition, the paint on the hood of her car had bubbled, and the vehicle was having electrical problems affecting the headlights and turn signal.

To make matters worse, the three women were ridiculed for sharing their story. These were churchgoing women who were respected in their community, not fantasy-prone individuals seeking publicity or profit. They had all led normal lives—until this happened. Louise Smith, a forty-four-year-old widow, worked for the Casey County Extension Office. Mona Stafford, who was divorced, owned an arts and crafts store and was doing secretarial work for her father, who operated a trailer park. Elaine Thomas was a fifty-three-year-old housewife.[10]

Some skeptics wanted to write the incident off as a shared delusion that started with one woman and was unwittingly embraced by the other two. This phenomenon is sometimes called *folie à deux*, or the foolishness of two. But Smith, Stafford, and Thomas weren't the only ones who saw UFOs in Casey and neighboring Lincoln County that January. Donna Coffey, who lived about a mile south of Hustonville, told Danville reporter Brenda Edwards that her family watched an unknown object in the sky for about two hours on January 6 and 19. "It had blue lights and would travel very fast for a time and then come back slowly. It would flash off and on, and at times there was a dim red light." Coffey said the object made no sound, appeared larger than a star, and might have been "thousands of miles away from earth."[11]

Greenewald reported that additional witnesses described a ring of reddish orange lights around a disc-shaped flying object. These corroborating descriptions make the Casey County Incident one of the better-documented cases of a UFO sighting and abduction. And such cases may be more common than we realize. According to paranormal researcher Coleman Larkin, the UFO Reporting Center estimates that thirty out of every one hundred thousand Kentuckians have seen some sort of aerial phenomenon. And that's just the number of people who have reported such cases.[12]

Of course, this doesn't necessarily mean that a nuts-and-bolts flying saucer actually appeared in the skies. UFO investigator Jerry Black says that 92 percent of UFO incidents are reported "by rattled witnesses [and the objects] turn out to be either aircraft, mistaken celestial bodies and other natural phenomena, or elaborate hoaxes."[13] Skeptics and UFO believers cite similar figures for the percentage of reports that remain unexplained. Still, that leaves 8 percent that can't be so easily debunked.

Given the distress caused by their experience, the three Liberty women were reluctant to relive the event. They initially rejected requests that they take polygraph tests or undergo regressive hypnosis to verify or clarify what really happened that fateful night. They hoped that, with time, their distress would disappear, like the flying object itself. But trauma doesn't work that way.[14] After two months of struggling with the aftermath of their experience, all three consented to be polygraphed and hypnotized. The *National Enquirer* offered to pay the expenses in exchange for exclusive rights to the women's story. Dr. Leo Sprinkle, a consultant to the science-based Aerial Phenomena Research Organization (APRO), conducted the regressive hypnosis sessions on March 7, 1976. Transcripts from those sessions suggest that something disturbing happened, but the women's recollections differed on many of the details.

Mona Stafford, the first to be hypnotized, recalled witnessing what appeared to be an imminent plane crash. This memory upset her so much that she started crying uncontrollably, so the session ended there. While Dr. Sprinkle questioned Louise Smith and Elaine Thomas under hypnosis, another interviewer showed Stafford drawings of aliens. This was apparently the first time the word "alien" was mentioned during the investigation.[15] After looking at the pictures, Stafford agreed that the drawings resembled a light she had seen and a face she recalled. But did they really? Or did the drawings influence her memories?

Since the women were so exhausted after their first hypnosis sessions, several months passed before they were hypnotized again on June 23, 1976, at the Brown Motel in Liberty. Meanwhile, the lie-detector tests were conducted by Lexington police detective James Young, an expert in the field but a skeptic when it came to UFOs. He tested each woman separately but in depth. The results were conclusive. To Young's "utter amazement," all three women "breezed through" the intensive test "without a hint of deception." The October 1976 issue of the *APRO Bulletin* notes that Young determined from the polygraph tests that "the ladies believed they were telling the truth to the listed questions," which focused on the UFO following the women on the highway rather than their abduction and examination.[16] That didn't surprise Mona Stafford (who later married and changed her last name to Floyd), who told the *Casey County News*, "We passed them all—nobody was able to shake our stories."[17]

More intensive regressive hypnosis sessions followed the polygraph tests. They were emotionally draining for the women and for anyone watching. "The details of what occurred on that harrowing night came slowly . . . hauntingly . . . painfully." The fear elicited by those captured memories was apparent from their "painful body contortions and movements," along with weeping, moaning, shuddering, and shaking. Dr. Sprinkle concluded: "All of the women were taken aboard some type of craft, and subjected to physical examinations, sometimes harsh in nature, sometimes tortuous. There was not any sexual molestation during the abduction, but they were restrained in embarrassing, humiliating positions."[18]

Under hypnosis, each woman recalled having her body scanned by several four-foot-tall "shadowy figures" with one or two eyes, but none of them mentioned a mouth. The figures floated or glided and communicated telepathically. Louise Smith's exam was apparently performed on a table, and Mona Stafford's was conducted in something resembling a chair. Greenewald reports that Elaine Thomas remembered being "inside a capsule with an unusual looking noose-like device around her neck, which tightened painfully if she tried to speak." Thomas also recalled "a tube with a bullet-like tip on it, which probed her chest." She mentioned a "deep darkness" in the room, while Stafford "could see a bright light at the end of a tunnel, which looked like a volcano with a jagged edge." It was hard for Stafford to see, though, because of the intense pain in her eyes. Jerry Black, who listened to eight hours of the emotionally charged sessions, said, "Mona had her eyes actually removed from her sockets, she claims, laid on her cheeks, and replaced again."[19]

Smith saw several different types of beings. Some appeared human, with hands that "looked like jagged wing tips." However, she was so scared that she kept her eyes closed and chose not to look at them. Stafford recalled seeing small figures dressed in white examining a helpless woman on a square table. She said the woman could have been Thomas, Smith, or even herself. Although the women claimed their arms and legs were twisted painfully, none reported that they were actually tortured.[20]

So, to summarize, we have a UFO, lost time, altered reality, medical consequences, and memories of being guinea pigs in alien experiments. What can we make of all this? As already noted, a shared delusion seems unlikely, given the additional eyewitness accounts of UFOs. Skeptics claim the women were tired after a day's work, followed by a long but pleasant dinner at the restaurant, and probably experienced highway hypnosis, a condition in which a car's occupants are lulled into a state of relaxed consciousness by the monotony of traveling along a dark highway. The travelers are not technically asleep, but they're in a little-understood and highly suggestible state in which they might remember waking dreams of aliens or flying saucers and confuse TV or Hollywood depictions with real events.

Scholars have studied highway hypnosis, including Gemma Pastor Cerezuela and colleagues, who reported in the journal *Accident Analysis and Prevention* that the reduced attention or alertness of highway hypnosis (as measured by eye movements) is more likely to develop on motorways or interstates, as opposed to standard highways.[21] By contrast, Shahram Rafieian and Steven Hosier characterize highway hypnosis as a "passive dissociative experience" that is "often seen secondary to another activity." They write, "An example of this kind of dissociation is daydreaming. Activities which are followed by passive dissociation are usual daily routines like taking a shower, jogging, and driving (highway hypnosis). When it happens, the person is absorbed by his or her internal world and becomes disconnected from place, time, and sense of self."[22] Affected individuals aren't necessarily out of touch with reality but simply "absorbed" in their thoughts. This occurs more often after hours of tedious driving on a freeway, not on a short trip along a two-lane rural road like Kentucky 78, which connects Stanford and Hustonville. The ten-mile stretch traverses rolling hills and has few straightaways, requiring drivers to stay alert. When we drove it recently, fifty-five miles per hour was the highest speed at which we felt safe—and only briefly. So highway hypnosis doesn't seem plausible. Plus, it doesn't explain the physical problems the women experienced such as burns, eye pain, and horrific headaches.

Many alien abduction reports collected from the 1980s through the early 2000s by researchers such as Bud Hopkins in New York and Dr. John Mack of Harvard were elicited through hypnotic regression. This method of retrieving information is controversial because it is possible for hypnotists to implant memories by asking leading questions or by making overt suggestions to the semiconscious but compliant participant. Upon waking, the witness "remembers" a detailed event that seems real but never actually occurred. Courts of law reject any evidence retrieved under hypnosis because those memories are considered unreliable and subject to outside suggestion.

Polygraphist James Young observed that earlier conversations the three Liberty women had about alien abduction with Dr. Sprinkle and a member of the Mutual UFO Network (believed to be Jerry Black) could have affected their memories. He said, "I cannot discount the fact that previous interviews with these persons could influence their personal beliefs as to whether or not this alleged encounter did or did not occur."[23] Believers argue that the three women were physically abducted by flesh-and-blood aliens. And even though others saw UFOs that night, they didn't witness the abduction, making it a less compelling possibility.

On a psychological level, the women's memories might stem from a waking dream in which they were experiencing an internal terror that's been part of the American psyche since colonial times. They may have unconsciously imagined themselves living out a trope from American literature: the captivity narrative. Similar captivity stories occur throughout world literature, but in the United States, with its history of racism, the fear of capture by a "Racial Other" takes on added energy. Americans have always feared being taken prisoner by aliens—not necessarily gray, interstellar aliens but the dreaded, misunderstood, and often hated Other, who may wield overwhelming power or influence. Examples of American captivity narratives include accounts by Captain John Smith of Jamestown, frontiersman Daniel Boone, Kentucky pioneer Jenny Wiley, and escaped slave Frederick Douglass. Dozens of examples exist, some from well into the twentieth century.

Experiences like the Casey County Incident have generated some pretty far-out theories. John A. Keel, author of *The Mothman Prophecies*, and UFO researcher Jacques Vallee have argued that transdimensional visitors, or perhaps time travelers, could account for many paranormal reports.[24] Did the three women glimpse shadows from another dimension? We love the multiverse concept, and the discussion in Vallee's work is intriguing, but little physical evidence supports this hypothesis. Perhaps we should limit our theories to our own universe of matter and energy. For example, each woman might have had a so-called frontal lobe cascade, a little-known cerebral event that can induce states of euphoria and hallucinations. This is a known phenomenon, but all three women experiencing this rare brain event at the same time is an extremely remote possibility.

Alien abduction? Unlikely.

Highway hypnosis? No way.

Mental episode? Rare in the extreme.

Hoax? To what end? The women did not profit from the incident and suffered ridicule for even reporting it.

This one's a stumper! We can propose no plausible explanation for this incident, so it remains an intriguing puzzle. Sadly, the women themselves never received any answers about their traumatic encounter or its meaning. Elaine Thomas was the first to pass away—just two and a half years after their alleged abduction. She died of an apparent heart attack in September 1978 at the age of fifty-six.[25] Although she had moved to Las Vegas, Louise Smith eventually returned to Kentucky and died in Hustonville in August 2003 at age seventy-one.[26] Mona Stafford Floyd died in Mt. Vernon in 2020 at age seventy-nine. Her memory of that fateful night in 1976 never faded. In September 2010 she said, "I see it now just as clear as I did 35 years ago."[27]

ALL ABOARD!

Did a Coal Train Collide with a UFO?

It was a chilly, dry night on January 14, 2002, when a CSX coal train reportedly collided with one of three UFOs somewhere north of Paintsville in far eastern Kentucky. The account reads like an *X-Files* episode. Here's what the unnamed engineer allegedly reported to his superiors at CSX headquarters the next day: "At exactly 2:47 a.m. . . . while working a coal train enroute from Russell, Kentucky [near Ashland], to Shelbiana, Kentucky [in Pike County, site of the state's second largest rail yard], our trailing unit and first two cars were severely damaged as we struck an unknown floating or hovering object. I know it was 2:47 because my watch froze, and to this day shows that time." The engineer said, "We hit the object at 30 mph with 16,000 trailing tons behind us." The object "clipped the top of our lead unit then skipped back slicing a chunk out of our trailing unit and first two coal cars. The other [two] objects vanished." In describing the "floating" object they hit, the engineer recalled that it was "metallic silver in color with multiple-colored lights near the bottom and in the middle. There were no windows or openings of any kind that we could see. It was 18-to-20-feet in length and probably 10-feet high."[1]

No one was injured in the incident, but both engines lost power. Understandably, the second engine failed after hitting the object, but the lead engine died as well. In fact, all the electrical equipment on the train malfunctioned for a few moments following the impact. Minutes later, the train's radio communications came back online, and the crew contacted their supervisors in Jacksonville, Florida, who told them to try to make it to the closest CSX facility—in Paintsville.

A mysterious "Mr. Ferguson" reportedly met the crew when the train limped into the rail yard at around 5:15 a.m. Crew members were then whisked away for intensive questioning by men who were definitely not railroad personnel. The crew reported seeing a flurry of activity under a large makeshift tent and heard "vehicle doors slamming, guys running by in weird outfits, and lights glaring from all directions."[2] Ultimately, the crew was drug-tested "for their own protection" and then returned to the CSX facility and released after being strongly cautioned not to talk about their mystifying experience—for national security reasons. After resting for eight hours in Shelbiana, the crew worked another train headed back to Russell. Before departing, they noticed that the damaged train's cars and engines and all the wreckage had been removed from the Paintsville yard as if nothing out of the ordinary had happened.

However, the crew couldn't forget that just hours earlier, something extraordinary *had* occurred: their train had been hit by a hovering UFO, their electronic devices had been temporarily knocked out, and men in black had arrived to debrief them, giving them strict orders not to talk about this uncanny encounter. Of course, someone did talk, putting the story out there for public consumption. Yet there's considerable doubt that this close encounter actually occurred.

Granted, the tale includes an actual time and date of the collision and a fairly specific location, but other than the mysterious Mr. Ferguson, no names were provided. And, as is the case with many paranormal events, attempts to confirm this story were derailed. We sent repeated inquiries to CSX's corporate public information office, Kentucky's Transportation Cabinet, and the Mutual UFO Network (MUFON) for details about the incident but received no responses. MUFON's silence is a significant red flag because it generally seizes any opportunity to discuss UFOs. This was a glaring exception.

Next, we checked local and state newspapers for reports of a train accident on January 14, 2002. There were no headlines and no photos—not even a one-inch mention on an inside page of any trouble involving a train that night. The dearth of news sends up another red flag.

We considered other explanations. For example, could something *resembling* a UFO have hit the train? An airplane or helicopter run-in would have been a matter of public record and reported in the local newspapers, but we found nothing. Since it was winter, perhaps a rogue slab of ice had damaged the train. Or it could have collided with low-hanging branches bowed down by snow or ice. According to Weatherspark.com, a database of historical weather information, Kentucky had a cold spell that week, but no rain, and temperatures that night were generally above freezing.[3] So these are not plausible explanations either.

The fact that the narrative provides no traceable names is a third red flag. Similar reports often contain witness statements along the lines of, "Please don't use my name because I'm afraid I'll lose my job." Understandably, some companies and organizations don't want to be linked to the UFO subculture. But the omission of witnesses' names may also indicate a hoax—with the fear of getting fired providing an all-too-convenient excuse for vague details. The railroad engineer, who was apparently too scared to reveal his name, divulged so much other information that any halfway competent corporate security officer could have easily discovered his identity. Withholding his name was pointless if he ultimately shared the whole story with the media anyway.

Also, even Uncle Sam's shadowy men in black would have had to work some high-performance magic to make a couple of damaged engines disappear into thin air in a matter of hours. It's a stretch to believe that they could hide all signs of a possible extraterrestrial incident should a reporter come snooping around the rail yard.

This alleged incident also sounds way too much like a script from *The X-Files*, which was still airing original episodes in the winter of 2002. Like FBI agents Fox Mulder and Dana Scully, we want to believe "the truth is out there," but in this case, we believe the truth is that the incident was a hoax—no doubt, case closed.

Still, just because this particular Kentucky UFO case was bogus doesn't mean that other UFO incidents aren't credible. Eastern Kentuckians apparently still see UFOs all the time. For example, in 2011 a large craft displaying pulsating red and green lights mystified observers in Greenup County near Ashland. According to a newspaper report:

> Linda Sargent said she was walking her dog, Jack, through Green Hill subdivision over a fresh snow under a clear sky shortly before 3 a.m. when she noticed "a real bright star. It looked bigger and it had an odd shape," Sargent said, noting she commented about the sight to her dog and continued to look at the curious object above her. "Then, all at once it just took off. Just whoosh . . . and it was gone." Sargent said the object in the sky seemed to travel straight up at an extremely high rate of speed and she is certain it could not have been any type of conventional aircraft. Sargent said she's certain she saw a UFO.[4]

The same article reported that Rachel Shelton and her husband saw a UFO near Cannonsburg (in Boyd County) after her son, Jeffrey Wheeler, insisted there was something bright in the dark clouds above them.

Seeing strange lights in the sky is fairly common. In fact, one Sunday night in late November about ten years ago, Mason observed a UFO passing over our house in Richmond. "I had just returned from the grocery," he said, "when I noticed a strange red light flickering through the leafless tree limbs. The intense ruby-colored light glittered like a laser pointer and flared into a star-shaped pattern from time to time. I watched as it moved slowly overhead—amazed at how silently it maneuvered." The light show lasted only a minute or two, and Mason didn't automatically jump to the conclusion that this was a flying saucer piloted by aliens. Yet, given the lack of sound and navigation lights, he didn't think it was a plane or a helicopter either.

Upon reflection, this sighting was likely the International Space Station passing overhead. Nevertheless, Mason reported the lights to MUFON and received a call back a few days later. The researcher went over the initial report and asked a series of follow-up questions, the most important one being: "Had you been drinking or using any controlled substances before your sighting?" He had not. At any rate, Mason's name is listed somewhere in the MUFON files for that Kentucky sighting in late November 2011 or 2012.

Most UFO cases fall into this same category: a witness reports strange lights in the sky, but there's a logical explanation once all the facts are considered. After all, we live in an age of increasing commercial, private, and military air travel. In fact, Spike Aerospace estimates that up to 500,000 persons are in the air at any given time and that up to six million persons fly on any given day.[5] We also live in an age of space exploration, which might account for some otherwise mysterious sightings like Mason's. In addition, today anyone can buy a radio-controlled drone—complete with camera—for less than $200, which likely accounts for a measurable percentage of current UFO reports.

As noted earlier, Carl Sagan suggested in *The Demon-Haunted World* that a lot of sincere UFO reports from the 1950s through the 1990s could be explained by the misidentification of covert Cold War weapons testing. And given the Cold War's atmosphere of secrecy and deception, the government would be unlikely to take any steps to reduce this confusion, preferring to let people think they've seen a UFO rather than scaring them with the reality of dangerous top-secret missile testing.

Keep in mind, too, that some atmospheric phenomena are still not fully understood, even by meteorologists. Thunderstorms, for example, can produce unusual, multicolored electrical displays called sprites. Observers have even reported rare clusters of red and orange sprites that resemble a jellyfish.[6] Depending on temperature and moisture content, the sky can reflect light in unusual ways, creating neatly colored patches called sun dogs on either side of the sun, as well as other anomalies. People can see lots of baffling things in the sky, none of which are alien spacecraft cruising through the neighborhood.

So what about the report of lights flitting around in a field near Morehead? University of Kentucky Professor Virgil Davis was driving home with his two teenaged sons between 9:00 and 10:00 p.m. on Friday, November 21, 2003. Here's how Kenny Young of the UFO Casebook website described the Morehead Incident:

> While driving, they all spotted a soundless aerial object over a nearby open field that was described as an oval-shaped, white-colored light source as big as a pea held at arm's length which moved "like a hummingbird would move." The object, seen in the dark and clear night skies, was relatively high when first seen and was "coming down, moving in increments as if an elevator would drop and stay there a while, and then drop and stay there a while," Davis said. After the first three or four minutes of visual observation, the object began moving around to different parts of the sky. They got out of the car to see if they could identify this object and verified to their satisfaction that the object was not a plane, helicopter, or aurora borealis.[7]

Once they arrived home, the three kept watching the object from a second-floor window. They saw it settle in a nearby field, where its color changed from white to orange. The object seemed to become slightly larger as it approached the ground, and then it became noticeably more reddish. "At this point, after the object got red, it just shot off like a dart to the west. We just stood there dumbfounded," Davis said.[8]

Shortly after the UFO's disappearance, the Davises heard the high-pitched sound of a woman screaming. They had been reluctant to phone the police about an apparently harmless aerial phenomenon, but human screams were a game changer. Officers who responded to the scene found nothing unusual in the field or in the area where the screams seemed to originate.

Although the case officially remains in the "unexplained" category, Christina Nunez, writing in *National Geographic,* believes the Morehead Incident was almost certainly an example of something called ball lightning: "Instances of ball lightning—glowing, electric orbs in the sky—have captivated and mystified us for centuries. The bizarre phenomenon, also known as globe lightning, usually [but not always] appears during thunderstorms as a floating sphere that can range from blue to orange to yellow, disappearing within a few seconds."[9]

Physicists have suggested that normal lightning strikes create millions of ionized air molecules, or plasma. This plasma then forms a sphere and floats for several seconds before dissipating—often with a bang or a hiss, or maybe what sounds like a woman's scream. According to Nunez, ball lightning may be related to lightning ground strikes, but there was no thunderstorm in the Morehead case. Other explanations include "air or gas behaving abnormally, high-density plasma phenomena, an air vortex containing luminous gases, and microwave radiation trapped within a plasma bubble."[10] None of these theories completely fits the observed phenomena of balls of energy floating in the sky.

Aviation journalist Philip J. Klass (1919–2005) famously made ball lightning his go-to explanation for almost all UFO cases with no other apparent cause. However, his critics have pointed out that he was using one poorly understood phenomenon, ball lightning, to explain another poorly understood phenomenon, UFOs. Jerome Clark notes that Klass was "out of his depth" in understanding the actual properties of ball lightning and that there is "considerable disparity between what plasmas look like and what UFO witnesses report."[11]

UFOs may not be nuts-and-bolts alien starships, as many believe, but they apparently possess enough physicality to show up in photos and on radar screens, and they occasionally leave traces on the ground. Right now, the physical evidence, as well as testimony from hundreds of credible witnesses including military personnel, law enforcement officers, and airline pilots, suggests that people are indeed seeing odd things in the sky. And although the government denies it has anything that can fly like the starship *Enterprise*, it might be more accurate to say that it has nothing *the public knows about* that can fly like that.

One objection to the idea that the US government possesses trailblazing technology is that it couldn't be kept secret. Inevitably, someone somewhere would blab about it. However, during World War II, the government ran the Manhattan Project in total secrecy—constructing the entire city of Oak Ridge, Tennessee, and hiding its real purpose of developing nuclear weapons even from the residents. We believe that certain government agencies are exceptionally good at keeping secrets—especially secrets that might involve world-dominating revolutionary technology.

And where did this technology come from? One of our favorite UFO legends is that the Americans and the Brits liberated some apocalyptic stuff from Nazi scientists at the end of World War II. Allied scientists have supposedly been testing something called field-repulsion technology ever since, which is why some very unconventional craft crashed in the late 1940s and 1950s. Is this system based on magnetism? An antigravity drive? The legend doesn't go into the engineering specifics. This narrative about captured Nazi "wonder weapons" is fascinating, but the evidence is sketchy.

On the subject of secret programs and sketchy rumors, we should mention the US "black budget." According to a Department of Defense (DOD) press release, its 2022 budget request included "$752.9 billion for national defense, $715 billion of which is for the DOD."[12] Of this amount, the Pentagon's black budget—funds earmarked for intelligence gathering and classified research and development—may exceed $50 billion a year.[13] Yet, in terms of accountability, nobody in the general public or in Congress knows what that vast river of money is flowing into. We suspect the US military can research and develop some immensely impressive weapons for $50 billion a year.

With that kind of funding, the United States might not need secondhand Nazi technology to build a groundbreaking flying machine. We've all heard rumors that military aviation is ten to twenty years ahead of civilian aviation—perhaps more. If this is true, current military vehicles being tested or even deployed might be unfamiliar to the average person and thus seem "alien." In fact, we would not be shocked to see "US Air Force" or "Royal Air Force" stenciled on the side of such a vehicle.

After a UFO lecture we gave several years ago, a man introduced himself to us as a recently retired US Air Force officer who had been stationed for years at Wright-Patterson Air Force Base near Dayton, Ohio. He said he couldn't disclose any information about current air force research projects but added, "Even if I *did* tell you what we're flying today, you wouldn't believe me anyway." Not believe him? Had he not been listening to the lecture? Although we were intrigued by his comment, we would need more evidence to draw accurate conclusions.

Finally, there is the comment made by aerospace engineer Ben Rich (1925–1995), the second director of Lockheed's Skunk Works research and development facility at Groom Lake, Nevada, also known as Area 51. Rich, along with his mentor Kelly Thompson, developed the F-104, the C-130, the U2 spy plane, the SR-71 Blackbird spy plane, and the F-117 stealth fighter, among other classified projects. Many of these top-secret craft were tested at the Groom Lake facility, more formally known as the Nevada Test and Training Range, administered by Edwards Air Force Base. Rich gave the UCLA School of Engineering alumni speech on March 23, 1993, and shared that researchers had solved a problem with their equations. "We've figured it out," he said, "and now we know how to travel to the stars, and it won't take a lifetime to do it." He continued, "We now have the technology to take E.T. back home."[14] Wow! Stay tuned. Who wouldn't want to book a seat on that flight?

Although strange craft are often seen flying over parts of Kentucky, it's highly unlikely that any of those UFOs originate from another star system. It is far more likely that they come from the Nevada Test and Training Range and the drawing boards of engineers like Ben Rich and Kelly Thompson. Or they might just be ball lightning.

CIVIL WAR GHOSTS

THE NEVER-ENDING STRUGGLE

Ghost Soldiers Still Fighting the Civil War

We drove into Perryville specifically looking for ghosts. We'd been told on good authority that the town was perhaps the most haunted spot in the commonwealth. Residents and visitors report spectral sightings almost daily. On the afternoon we visited, however, we encountered no specters, but we did hear some very creepy ghost stories.

Perryville is a small town of 964 residents (according to the 2020 census), resting nearly halfway between Danville and Springfield along US 150. It has been a quiet place ever since a band of settlers from Virginia arrived in January 1781, with one exception: October 8, 1862. On that day, the largest Civil War battle in Kentucky erupted in the open fields west and north of town. The battle was brutal, even by Civil War standards. Casualties numbered in the thousands—7,621 to be exact. So there's no shortage of spirits left to wander the battlefield.

Historically, the battle's outcome affected the entire war because the Confederates squandered an opportunity to put the North on the defensive. Civil War reenactors regularly return to Perryville to interpret those few crucial hours. We have attended several reenactments and found them to be an exciting immersive experience. Spectators jump at the impact of the cannon fire, cringe at the roar of muskets, smell the stifling smoke as it wafts through the air, and picture the soldiers battling at close range using bayonets and clubbed muskets.

In a 2012 interview, historian Kenneth Noe observed that both commanders at Perryville misunderstood what was happening during their chance encounter, resulting in "shock, confusion, and hard fighting" when the enemy appeared "seemingly out of nowhere." Noe noted that because of the landscape and desperate circumstances, death by "friendly fire" was common. "Ultimately, the Confederate attack required men to fight uphill all afternoon, over one ridge, and then another, no easy task in hot and dry weather, while the Federal defenders effectively used the same hills to their advantage." Perryville is "one of the nation's best-preserved battlefields," according to Noe.[1]

Today's vista is more or less what the soldiers saw in 1862, according to the Kentucky State Parks website. In many ways, it's a typical battlefield park with a Visitors Center, walking trails, and interpretive signs. What is not typical, however, is that visitors often report being accompanied on the trails by one or more soldiers who may look like reenactors but are outfitted in absolutely authentic Civil War garb. While the modern-day visitors go home at the end of their adventurous day, their spirited companions never leave the battlefield where they fell.

Kentucky authors Bryan Bush and Thomas Freese recount the following story, titled "Call to the Line," in their 2010 book *Haunted Battlefields of the South*: One night in the mid-1980s a reenactor named Barry arrived early for the annual Perryville event. He set up his tent on the battlefield just before a heavy storm, and later that night he was awakened by someone tugging on his pants leg. Still groggy, Barry noticed a Confederate soldier squatting outside his tent, his rifle propped up against him and raindrops dripping off the brim of his hat. "He wants you up there," the soldier said, pointing away from the tent. Barry had no idea who the soldier was, where he'd come from, or what he was talking about. *Who* wanted him? Where was *up there*? And what was so important that he had to be summoned at this hour, since the reenactment wasn't scheduled to start until later the next day? Outside the tent, it was too dark to tell where the soldier was pointing. The soldier then repeated his message, "He wants you up there." Then he leaned into the tent and handed his rifle to Barry, saying, "Here, you might need this." According to Bush and Freese, Barry "climbed out of his sleeping blanket to look around the tent. There was not a soul in sight, not even the back of a prankster walking away."[2] Eerily, the night before, members of Barry's battalion had heard shouted commands, horses running at full gallop, and rifle fire, even though a park ranger assured the reenactors that they were the only campers present that evening.

Apparitions like this are relatively rare, however. Many hauntings are simply unrecognizable sounds or shadowy figures glimpsed out of the corner of an eye. Barry's encounter consisted of a full-body apparition that delivered an audible message. A "noisy ghost," or poltergeist, is a much more interactive form of haunting than a specter—a visible disembodied spirit that haunts the mind. In contrast, a poltergeist can make loud noises, move or destroy objects, set fires, or even torment individuals by pinching, biting, hitting, or tripping them.

For a quiet town, Perryville has quite a collection of noisy ghost sightings. "We see and hear battlefield sights and sounds almost every day, so we're used to it and don't pay attention to it half the time," Bryan Bush told us in a July 2022 interview at the Perryville Visitors Center, which displays Civil War artifacts and maps of the battlefield. Besides being an author and reenactor, Bush is the park manager there. "We hear rifle and cannon fire even in the daytime," he said, and once he heard a drum roll that sounded like it came from the cemetery.

Civil War reenactors seem to encounter more than their share of apparitions. "When we dress in uniform and in period attire, something often happens. I think during reenactments, they [the spirits] see someone like them so they come up and want help," Bush said. One locus for paranormal activity seems to be the Visitors Center, whose foundation was constructed from stones recycled from a Civil War–era structure called the Yankee House. Paranormal investigators have suggested to Bush that the stones carry the "latent vibrations" of a few lost souls. The building is also close to a Confederate mass grave and a monument erected to recognize the Southern soldiers' sacrifice.

Some of the reported encounters are more solid than mere vibrations. A prankster spirit, believed to be a Civil War drummer boy, supposedly haunts the Visitors Center restrooms, where the doors stick, taps turn on and off by themselves, and voices are heard when no living person is present. The drummer boy was also seen on a chilly day hanging around a group of reenactors' early morning campfire as they were cooking breakfast. The Bush-Freese book describes him as twelve or thirteen years old, wearing "a Confederate gray kepi, gray wool pants, and a white muslin shirt." He sat quietly near the warm fire and then stood in line for food once it was ready. However, having never uttered a word, he disappeared before filling his plate. The reenactors assumed he had just walked away, but no one remembered him leaving. Drummer boys were often casualties of war, since they were stationed on the battlefront, signaling orders with their drumbeats. "Unfortunately, many of them were severely wounded or killed, crying for their mothers as they breathed their last breath upon the earth," Bush said.

Understandably, the most vivid manifestations occur on the battlefield itself. Bush and Freese cite reenactor Terrell Bryant, who participated in the 140th anniversary of the battle in 2002. Bryant and several others witnessed what was apparently a phantom artillery crew drilling near a cannon on Heart

Attack Hill. The witnesses were standing by the monument in the middle of the park, waiting for the artillery reenactors to perform a night firing, when Bryant and the others noticed that a gun crew was already drilling up on the hill. The sun was setting, backlighting the cannon crew as the men performed their maneuvers. "It looked like they were loading and shooting the cannons," Bryant said. "But they weren't really shooting anything—we didn't hear or see the cannons go off. They were just going through the maneuvers. They were just practicing to get ready for shooting. We watched them go through the maneuvers a couple of times when we saw a group of spectators who walked up the hill toward the cannons. We watched them get up to the cannons and then the cannon crew just vanished into midair." Bryant ended his story by saying, "I think the ghosts see the reenactors in uniform and they feel like it's a little easier to let down their guard."[3]

When the crew of the Travel Channel's *Ghost Adventures* visited Perryville (season 8, episode 13, air date November 15, 2013), host Zak Bagans reported hearing cannon fire while doing a nighttime investigation. The sound was loud enough to be captured by the crew's microphones. The show's producers couldn't identify any reason for an explosion to be heard in the area that night.

On a somewhat darker note, Bush told us about a couple who visited the battlefield several years ago. The husband, who was sensitive to psychic events, said he felt the presence of Confederate spirits—and they were "really mad." According to the psychic, the spirits weren't mad about being dead. They had other unresolved complaints. After the battle, local residents buried some 444 Confederate soldiers in two mass burial pits in the park. "No one knows their names, who they are," the psychic told Bush, "and the soldiers don't know why they can't go home."

If the lost Confederates are upset, at least they don't take out their anger on the park's visitors or employees. "We've never had anything threatening happen here," Bush said. "People just report seeing a soldier walking picket duty, or hear voices, or occasionally hear a musket shot or cannon fire." One typical story concerns a new Perryville resident who was walking downtown along Merchant's Row and happened to look through the front window of a store that had been used as a hospital after the battle. He saw a man dressed in a Union officer's uniform, filling out paperwork by lamplight. "He described the figure's hat," Bush said. "It had 'M.S.' on it, for 'Medical Service.' Apparently, he was a Union surgeon." That building and many others served as emergency field hospitals to treat the wounded on both sides of the war. "How horrible to be doing medical paperwork for the rest of eternity," Bush noted.

A few years ago, KET's *Kentucky Life* broadcast a documentary about Bluegrass ghosts, including this story: One summer evening, a young woman and her friend were sitting on the porch of the H. P. Barnum house in Perryville. The two women were chatting quietly by the light of a Coleman lamp when a man dressed in a Confederate uniform suddenly approached them from the field. The women naturally thought he was a reenactor involved in some historically accurate live-action role playing (known as LARP-ing). "Ladies," the soldier said politely but firmly, "the lamp will give away our position." Then he turned and slowly dematerialized into the darkness.[4] It's an eerie story, mainly because of the figure's disappearing act. Like Barry's encounter, this one seems to involve a snippet of dialogue captured from the battle itself. The words aren't spooky or threatening, but they're strange because they sound so real—like something a Civil War soldier might have said in 1862. The spirits "are not necessarily interacting with us," Bush told us. "It's more like they're speaking to someone from a previous life. They're just repeating what was said earlier—and they go through the motions like a broken record."

Mason earned his undergraduate degree from Centre College in Danville, just ten miles from Perryville. The college's administration building, Old Centre, was used as a hospital after the battle, and its floors, now covered with carpet, are said to still bear bloodstains. Centre students also tell stories about motorists driving along US 150 late at night who report seeing groups of wounded soldiers in Civil War uniforms hobbling toward the medical facilities in Danville. But when the motorists stop to offer help, the soldiers have vanished. Partly because of stories like these, Perryville has earned its reputation as "spook central" (as Dan Aykroyd said of a haunted location in the 1984 movie *Ghostbusters*).

Leslie Kean, in her 2017 book *Surviving Death*, cites Erlendur Haraldsson of the University of Iceland, who spent years researching after-death communications. Haraldsson's numbers suggest that "persons suffering a violent death feature predominantly in cases of apparitions of the dead and in cases of the reincarnation type, as well as in mediumship, including both direct communicators and drop-ins. The cases tend to have an invasive character, in that the deceased persons are frequently unknown to those who experience them and thus seem to assume an active role in their appearance. All of these findings tend, in my view, to support the survival hypothesis."[5]

If violent deaths play a role in why specters stick around, no wonder visitors to Perryville are occasionally joined by a battered soldier as they hike around the battlefield. On the other hand, a skeptic would argue that battlefields attract hundreds of authentically outfitted reenactors every year. These reenactors don't always know one another, but they have amassed more Civil War lore than the average person. As we discovered while talking with an accurately attired group at an encampment in Perryville, some reenactors are sticklers for details—insisting that even the buttons on their uniforms be sewn on in proper nineteenth-century fashion. These guys look like the real deal—from spectacles to boots. So, if an unknown figure on the battlefield looks like a soldier and acts like a soldier he is probably a reenactor—not a ghost still wandering the battlefield 160-plus years later.

Now, let's scrutinize the "vanishing into thin air" comment. This disappearing act might be easier to pull off than it seems. Interestingly, many outspoken skeptics once pursued the art of stage magic in their younger years. Early twentieth-century magician Harry Houdini and, more recently, Penn Jillette, half of the magical duo Penn & Teller, and Joe Nickell of the *Skeptical Inquirer* are examples of people trained in stage magic who have denounced hoaxes and other paranormal deceptions. These performers know that it isn't hard to trick people because audience members *want* to be fooled. For example, by using misdirection—flourishing one hand to draw spectators' attention while removing a card or coin from a pocket with the other hand—magicians can amaze an audience. Illusions like this don't even require special props.

The "Disappearing Woman Trick," for example, doesn't require a fancy display box with a concealed panel that the magician's assistant climbs into onstage. The assistant can seem to disappear simply by stepping out of the center-stage spotlight and into the shadows upstage. The assistant, who might be wearing highly reflective clothing and a dark cape, simply steps into the darkness, turns to present the dark cape to the audience, and abracadabra! The spectators' glare-adjusted eyes see the assistant vanish. Poof! She's gone. Sometimes a puff of stage smoke helps hide the otherwise obvious exit.

Stage illusions are harmless fun and games, but Civil War battles were not. The terrible truth is that when young men disappeared in a puff of smoke during the Perryville battle, they didn't reappear from behind a curtain or a hidden panel. They never came back. A reenactor, however, might step into the darkness just outside the cone of light from a Coleman lantern and effectively—though not necessarily intentionally—dissolve into thin air.

The armies came to Perryville in the summer of 1862 because of a drought. The men desperately needed water. So, this was an almost accidental battle in which 4,220 Union and 3,401 Confederate soldiers died, were wounded, or went missing. The actual body count was 1,422 dead and 5,534 wounded. These numbers are close to the historian's rule of thumb that for every battlefield death in the Civil War, four soldiers were wounded. Of the wounded, 955 of them later died, bringing the death toll to 2,377.[6]

After the shooting stopped, Confederate General Braxton Bragg abandoned the field, leaving Southern dead and wounded to whatever fate awaited them. With too many bodies to bury separately, local farmers dug mass graves on their own property. Of the 444 Confederate bodies buried in mass graves near the Perryville Visitors Center, only 33 have been identified, according to Bryan Bush. Some 869 Union bodies were later moved to Camp Nelson National Cemetery near Nicholasville and reinterred there. Roughly 200 of those soldiers remain unidentified.

With so many young men dying so violently so far from home, it's no wonder that Perryville is considered one of the most haunted places in Kentucky, according to travel journalist Andrea Limke. She includes the town of Perryville too, not just the battlefield. Limke notes that during paranormal tours of Perryville, people report "seeing full-bodied apparitions, hearing the sounds of marching when no one else is around, and disembodied voices" in various buildings.[7]

It seems that the people of Perryville take these paranormal accounts in stride. Their ancestors might have passed along stories about the 1862 battle that left bloodstains in buildings and emotional scars on civilians who were pressed into service as caregivers. In the KET documentary, Vicki Goode, executive director of Main Street Perryville, said some homes carry lasting reminders of the soldiers who stayed there. "It was typical for them to write their name, their rank, and where they were from" on the walls, Goode says, so they wouldn't be forgotten. Goode isn't worried about Perryville having a "haunted reputation." She says, "We have a wealth of history, and the hauntings are part of that history."

As author Colin Dickey notes, telling ghost stories helps us process historical events that may be too painful to describe in normal terms. We reenact in fiction what we can't articulate in real life. After all, issues raised by the Civil War still echo today in politics, culture, and regional identities.[8]

All that suffering. All that blood. All those deaths. The Civil War's horrors still haunt the dreams of Americans today.

SEARCHING FOR WRAITHS IN ALL THE WRONG PLACES

The Battle of Richmond and Camp Nelson

When a place *looks* like it should be haunted but has no paranormal activity attached to it, people sometimes just make up a resident ghost. After all, what's the harm in a bit of hometown mythmaking?

We encountered several such places during our Kentucky research. For example, there's Battlefield Park on US 421 (Battlefield Memorial Highway), a few miles south of Richmond and across from the Blue Grass Army Depot. We've been there many times to watch Civil War reenactors depict the Battle of Richmond, with soldiers on horseback engaging in sword fights, troops marching across a hilly field to confront the enemy, cannons being fired that make your body shake and your ears ring, and soldiers driving a wagon onto the field to collect the wounded. There are walking trails and picnic tables on the park grounds, and several "witness structures" are still standing. Those nearby structures include the Mount Zion Church, which served as a hospital during and after the 1862 battle, and the Rogers House, which was "literally surrounded by some of the most intense fighting during the Civil War in Kentucky." It became a makeshift hospital, ended up "hosting troops from both sides," and now houses the battlefield's Visitors Center.[1]

Except for the August reenactment, the battlefield is quiet, at least in paranormal terms, with no apparitions reported on the grounds or in any of the witness structures. That's disappointing news for ghost hunters because hundreds of soldiers died at the Battle of Richmond, second only to Perryville in the number of casualties. Many deaths must mean many spirits, right? Not necessarily.

One paranormal group called R&S Exploring posted a five-minute video in May 2023 following a nighttime investigation at the battlefield. They hashtagged the video #ghost, #haunted, #paranormal, #scary, #paranormal activity, #ghosthunters, #creepy, #ghost hunting, and #cemetery, so naturally we were expecting spooky things, but it was basically false advertising. The group shared scenes from the park, including shots of an old barn on the property and Pleasant View House, which was vacant during the fighting because the residents had fled, but the house showed signs of artillery damage. The soundtrack consisted of ominous horror-movie music, but no ghosts appeared. Several small, tantalizing light streaks can be seen on the video, but these were most likely caused by lightning bugs, not ectoplasmic apparitions.[2]

Richmond was one of thirteen Civil War battles fought in Kentucky, including Mill Springs, Munfordville, Cynthiana, Somerset, Lebanon, Barbourville, Paducah, and, of course, Perryville. The two-day Battle of Richmond (August 29–30, 1862) was a massive Confederate victory and a precursor to the bloody Battle of Perryville. "Of the 7,000 Federal troops engaged, only about 500 escaped the Confederate onslaught," according to an article posted on the Madison County website.[3] The majority of these casualties were Union troops captured by the Confederates. Fewer than five hundred men were killed in action at Richmond, and about one thousand were wounded.[4]

What began as a skirmish developed into an artillery duel and then infantry combat. The engagement started about seven miles south of Richmond near the present-day Blue Grass Army Depot and Mount Zion Church. As Union forces retreated, the battle spread to a plot of land where a middle school now stands, then extended to the Richmond Cemetery. Finally, the retreating Union soldiers fled through the town itself before most of them were rounded up and captured.[5]

So, with all that action, are there any actual Battle of Richmond ghosts in our midst? Possibly. One apparently appeared in Lexington a century ago. In *Haunted Houses and Family Ghosts of Kentucky*, William Lynwood Montell shares a story from a newspaper article published in the late nineteenth or early twentieth century. The tale concerns an old brick house in Lexington where a Union soldier, mortally wounded at Richmond, was taken for treatment. Soon after he died of his wounds, the apparitions began. Residents reported hearing deep groans coming from the front room of the house—perhaps where the soldier spent his final days. Years later a young family moved in, presumably unaware of the house's history. In classic ghost-tale fashion, they were eating dinner one night when suddenly the gas lamps went out and groans were heard from the front room. Out of the darkness, a man wrapped in gauze bandages appeared and raised his arms, displaying an open chest wound. The family gaped in horror, unable to move. Montell reports that the apparition lasted only a moment, but that was long enough. The traumatized family moved out the next day.[6]

Montell says of this story and others like it: "These accounts of spirit visitation grip the listeners, and especially the tellers, with genuinely uncanny power. Most of these gripping, spooky stories are believed from the heart, even when logical rationale would assert that what is being described did not happen."[7] At least Montell is honest about the vagueness of this story. The original reporter didn't name the families who lived in the house or the soldier who died; nor was the Lexington address given. So it's a chilling tale to tell around the campfire—but little else.

From fireside fantasy to fact: Mount Zion Church still has a cannonball embedded in the south wall from the Battle of Richmond. The Disciples of Christ have held services there since 1852. We have attended services at the church during the battle's reenactment weekends and when Civil War–themed speakers portray characters from that period. The building is a suitable venue for these programs, as army surgeons performed assembly-line amputations at the church-turned-hospital. Poorly staffed and supplied, the tired and most likely distraught medical staff simply tossed the severed limbs out the window until the pile of arms, legs, and other body parts reached the windowsill. Images like this are impossible to erase from our minds. No wonder Civil War stories haunt us at 3:00 a.m. on sleepless nights—even without any visitations from spirits.

Phillip Seyfrit, curator of the Battle of Richmond Visitors Center, told us in an August 2022 interview that he has received very few reports of paranormal activity at the site. And he's okay with that because it keeps the spotlight on the historical value of the battle itself. Besides, any gunfire or explosions that might be heard would hardly be considered paranormal. The park is located next to the Blue Grass Army Depot—a storage facility that sometimes disposes of obsolete or damaged military ordinance by detonating it. Such activity isn't only loud; it can also shake nearby houses.

According to Seyfrit, the only supernatural report he remembers came from a woman who lived in neighboring Battlefield Estates. She claimed she could hear troops marching through the night but didn't specify whether she heard marching feet or drums and music. Despite the lack of paranormal reports, about a third of the visitors ask Seyfrit about ghosts. And some of the tourists come prepared to check for spirits themselves. "We had a woman come in a few years ago who was looking at the exhibits downstairs and took out some kind of device and started moving around the lower floor," Seyfrit told us. "She started up the stairs and let out a whoop. The device was a 'ghost detector,' she said, and it had given her the strongest reading she'd ever seen." Although this particular ghost hunter was excited by her results, Seyfrit said, "I've never seen or heard anything unusual in here." The building's spirits, if they exist, must be on the shy side.

Just because a site is quiet in the *paranormal* sense doesn't mean that it's quiet *physically*. Seyfrit noted that the Visitors Center (formally the Rogers House) is obviously an old structure. "It makes a lot of noise—all old houses do." But the various pops and groans don't necessarily come from restless spirits. Houses, even old ones, are best thought of as engines, as Tracy Kidder argues in his 1999 book *House*.[8] Energy flows over them and through them in the form of electricity, heating and cooling, water, and wind. An old wooden house is much like a ship at sea—groaning and creaking with the pressure of wind and water. Not every rasp on the stairway at midnight is a phantom's footstep. After all, how much could a ghost weigh? It's more likely a sound generated by the normal cooling and contracting of the house at night.

Another off-site ghost report came from a Reddit.com respondent, "Spooky2066," who posted the following story about a haunting that developed long after the 1862 battle:

> I live in a house that was built along the trail taken from the battlefield outside of Richmond, Ky. to the battlefield of Perryville. We constantly have things happen here, from doors opening themselves to unembodied footsteps. Loud banging to wine bottles flying off the rack. We had a psychic come and see what she thought was going on. She informed us that we had a Confederate soldier who died from injuries on the march from the Battle of Richmond. I have never seen him, but he makes his presence known all of the time. He's a part of the family now.[9]

The highway that connects Richmond and Perryville is Kentucky 52, which runs through Kirksville, Paint Lick, and Danville. It's heavily traveled day and night by cars and trucks, and the vibrations could make an old structure shake, causing doors to open by themselves. This wouldn't be the first "haunting" produced by an eighteen-wheeler.

It's worth noting that the only connection between this report and the Battle of Richmond comes from the unnamed psychic. Sketchy as the attribution is, for the sake of argument, let's assume that Spooky2066's report is a genuine manifestation. Why would the spirit suddenly start appearing more than 150 years after the battle? Perhaps the current family harbors "Northern sympathies," causing the angry wraith in gray to slam doors and toss wine bottles around.

Another questionable off-battlefield haunting is recorded in Alan Brown's *Kentucky Legends and Lore.* Brown reports that Sullivan Hall at Eastern Kentucky University, built in 1912, sits on the site of a field hospital erected after the battle. The argument goes that because so many soldiers died at that location, Sullivan Hall, although constructed decades after the war, is still haunted by their spirits. Though this explanation may sound plausible, it seems to be a variation on the narrative of ghosts haunting buildings that occupy Native American burial grounds. Brown cites no source for the story.[10]

Besides the Perryville and Richmond battlefields, if any Civil War site in Kentucky *should* be haunted, it's Camp Nelson National Monument, a 525-acre park near Nicholasville where thousands of Union soldiers are buried (no Confederates allowed). According to the National Cemetery Administration, the camp played an important role in supplying the US Army with provisions, wagons, ambulances, and artillery equipment, as well as caring for the sick and wounded at its seven hundred–bed hospital. By 1868, some 2,023 Union dead had been moved to Camp Nelson National Cemetery.[11]

The camp also recruited and trained new soldiers for the Union, including about ten thousand Black men—formerly enslaved African Americans—who volunteered to serve with the US Colored Troops.[12] They weren't always welcomed because it was a radical idea to enlist formerly enslaved men and train them to fight. In Danville, "citizens threw stones and shot pistols at 250 Black recruits." And in Taylor County, "some recruits were beaten and thrown in jail."[13]

The Black soldiers' families who accompanied them also suffered when the military failed to consider their well-being. At one point, four hundred families were forced to leave their shanty village in freezing temperatures and fend for themselves. As a result, 102 individuals died from exposure and disease. Outraged, the *New York Tribune* published a front-page article on November 28, 1864, headlined: "Cruel Treatment of the Wives and Children of U.S. Colored Soldiers." The newspaper criticized the army's harsh decision to evict family members who "are now lying in barns and mule sheds, wandering through the woods . . . literally starving, for no other crime than their husbands and fathers having thrown aside the manacles of Slavery to shoulder Union muskets." Within a month, the military changed course and began building "cottages for families, a mess hall, barracks, a school, teachers' quarters, and a dormitory." Although that was remarkable progress, diseases such as smallpox, measles, chronic diarrhea, dysentery, and typhoid fever caused by "overcrowded conditions and poor sanitation, especially the contamination of water," claimed thirteen hundred lives.[14]

Like Richmond, Camp Nelson is quiet in the supernatural sense, with only sporadic reports of people walking and talking when no one's there, lights inexplicably turning on and off in the museum, and a ghost-like vision in a window. So where's the best place to see a real Civil War ghost?

In 2021 we viewed the Louisville Speed Museum's exhibit *Supernatural America: The Paranormal in American Art*, which included several sections created by Civil War veterans. With two hundred objects on view, it was the Speed's largest display ever. The exhibit was divided into four parts: America as a Haunted Place, Apparitions, Channeling Spirits/Rituals, and Plural Universes.

Marie wrote in her *Richmond Register* column on December 18, 2021, that there were paintings of restless spirits, unsettled ghosts, and unresolved conflicts. Many dealt with war scenes, with one sign noting, "Lingering spirits can't resolve the troubling issues that traumatized them." Union soldier James Henry Beard, an eyewitness to the personal devastation of the war, painted the haunting *The Night before the Battle* in 1865. "The painting portrays two armies from the same side—one living, the other dead," Marie writes. "The living soldiers are trying to rest before engaging the enemy the next day. But they realize they could be killed in a matter of hours, so they've pinned their names to their clothes so their bodies can be identified. A skeleton soldier stands near a cannon, ready to light the fuse and begin the battle which will claim so many lives."[15] Another work on display was a "spirit painting," where the artist, in a trance-like state, lets the spirit control his or her hands to create a piece of art.

Victims of the Civil War still haunt our art, our literature, and our popular culture—if not our battlefields. These ghosts appear in countless movies, novels, and videos, as well as certain battlefield parks.

The evidence for ghosts being actual disembodied spirits of departed human beings—so-called ectoplasm—is hardly compelling. Such evidence consists almost entirely of eyewitness accounts, which are unconvincing without physical corroboration. Unfortunately, physical evidence is rare indeed. Researching this phenomenon is made more difficult by hoaxes, misidentifications, and folktale motifs that fill our minds whenever we see an old run-down house that looks like it could be haunted. That being said, people apparently do see some eerie things from time to time. Some of these unusual sights are not easy to explain, especially when they occur in places that have witnessed massive death and destruction—like battlefields—and they merit further review.

But if ghosts do exist, spirits from sites like Richmond and Perryville might find comfort in resting with their comrades in a place of honor, such as national cemeteries like Camp Nelson or on the battlefields themselves. There, they lie surrounded by natural beauty and in a spot where their bravery is remembered—recited every day to visitors, tourists, and school groups. Today, children laugh and play near the fields. Middle-aged birders with binoculars search the trees for rare species. Young lovers stroll hand in hand in the shade. Reenactors camp in the same valleys and march over the same roads. What better place for Civil War soldiers to rest?

Ghost hunters get it wrong when they try to make spirits speak. Instead, we should tell the fallen warriors that their actions created the nation we inherited. If we could somehow reach them, how would we convey that message to these ghostly battalions? How could we assure them that America remains worthy of their sacrifice? We'd like to believe that if we could stand over the graves at Richmond, Camp Nelson, Perryville, and other battle sites, and if there was any consciousness there to hear us, we could say, like the title character in Steven Spielberg's *Saving Private Ryan*: "I've tried to live my life the best I could. I hope that was enough. I hope that, at least in your eyes, I've *earned* what all of you have done for me."[16]

CIVIL WAR CASUALTIES

Soldiers' Spirits Occupy Octagon Hall

It's not hard to spot the next site on our haunted house hit parade: Octagon Hall in Franklin, about thirteen miles south of Bowling Green. The distinctive eight-sided home sits on 1.8 acres along US 31W like an isolated medieval castle. There's no moat, curtain wall, or drawbridge, but like many European castles, Octagon Hall is said to harbor ghosts. It is often listed as one of the most haunted places in Kentucky, which seems odd for this beautiful structure in such a tranquil rural landscape.

Andrew Jackson Caldwell didn't intend for his home to become a ghost hotel when he started building the unusual three-level brick house in 1847. It was completed twelve years later, just a year before the Civil War broke out. Caldwell, a high-ranking Mason, may have chosen the octagonal shape to represent a Masonic symbol of rebirth and resurrection. It's also supposed to attract positive energy from all eight directions. As a bonus, Caldwell found that the design both deflected winds and captured breezes (long before air-conditioning), and it afforded great views of a major road leading to Bowling Green.

No Civil War battles were fought on the property, but the Caldwell home's strategic location near the L&N Railroad line provided convenient transportation as well as a perfect observation post and a handy campsite. Those advantages drew troops from both sides like a magnet. As an active Southern sympathizer, Andrew Caldwell was considered an enemy of the Union. He often hid Confederate soldiers, spies, or guerrillas in hollow closets and several secret tunnels located throughout his house. These concealed areas could be accessed through trapdoors, rope ladders, and discreet passageways. Long-lost coins, buttons, and suspenders have been discovered in these spots. The family even dressed some soldiers in beekeeper suits and hid them among the beehives in the cupola, where Union troops were unlikely to look for them.[1]

Through these efforts, some Confederate soldiers escaped capture by Union officers who suspected Caldwell of harboring the traitors and conducted regular searches of the premises. Others, though well hidden, were too sick or badly injured and died while awaiting medical treatment. Perhaps this failed humanitarian effort is one reason for the hodgepodge of "haints" and paranormal investigators swarming through the house, including teams representing the Travel, History, and Discovery Channels.

On February 13, 1862, the Confederates were the first to arrive at Octagon Hall. Southern forces had suffered major defeats at Forts Henry and Donelson in Tennessee, and the South was in full retreat. Some nine thousand soldiers, many of them wounded and sick, had been marching about twenty miles a day in the cold, and they were in terrible physical and mental shape when they reached Franklin.[2] After only one night's rest, the Confederates had to move on, and they left many of the injured behind. The Caldwells did what they could to protect those Confederate soldiers. They converted the house's second floor into a hospital area to treat the wounded, but most of the crude amputations of arms, legs, and hands took place in the basement.

With all the violence, injuries, and death connected to the Caldwell home, it seems logical that Octagon Hall has been deemed a "sanctuary for the supernatural," where witnesses have reported both seeing and feeling spirits.[3] We visited the place on a quiet July afternoon in 2022, when there was plenty of sunshine bathing the house and its surroundings. So it's not surprising we didn't notice any apparitions floating around. Haunted houses tend to live up to their reputations at 2:00 a.m. rather than 2:00 p.m.

Museum director Barry "Bear" Gaunt, who has been associated with the hall for forty-six years, greeted us at the door, provided an hour-long history of the house, and then turned us loose on a self-guided tour. Gaunt says they've counted about two hundred different spirits hanging around. Paranormal groups have sent the museum six thousand images that capture ghostly activities, as well as recorded sounds that are open to interpretation.

A 2021 *Kentucky Monthly* article notes that witnesses have seen shadow figures and full-body apparitions of uniformed Civil War soldiers. Unearthly voices have been captured on special equipment brought for that very purpose.[4]

Bethany Ford, a member of the Uncommon in the Commonwealth paranormal team that investigated Octagon Hall, was surprised by how active the spirits were during their 2020 visit. They found the basement kitchen to be the eeriest place in the house. "It was spooky and creepy, and you felt an overwhelming sense of dread."[5]

The Caldwell family paid a price for their support of the Confederacy. According to Gaunt, two days after the Confederates' departure in 1862, the Union army camped on the grounds and stayed for several weeks, interrogating and torturing Caldwell and his wife and possibly mistreating prisoners. Gaunt said the Yankees' persecution of Southern sympathizers "ripped the souls out of people."

During our visit, Gaunt told us a story about the brutal violence inflicted on Mrs. Caldwell, which we were unable to verify. He says a Union officer cut off her hand while she was trying to help a housemate. In a family photograph displayed in the house, the Caldwells are sitting together in a typical nineteenth-century pose: staring stiffly at the camera. Mrs. Caldwell's left hand, which is partly tucked out of sight, appears oddly straight and discolored. "That's her wooden hand," Gaunt explained.

Octagon Hall, which is filled with Confederate artifacts such as old uniforms, battle flags, and various weapons, has one lingering spirit—a lonely Confederate soldier known only as Eddie, who hangs out in the attic where he died. He was shot outside the house by a Union soldier, dashed inside, climbed up to the attic, and hid. Unfortunately, it took three days for the Union army to leave, and by the time the Caldwells were able to check on him, Eddie was dead. In more recent times, when he's in the mood, Eddie apparently communicates with paranormal investigators, who record the conversations. Eddie's ghostly footsteps are distinguishable from others because they sound "like he's dragging his leg."[6]

Throughout the war the Caldwells continued to be harassed by the Union army. According to Gaunt, Union forces butchered the family's cattle and sent the meat via railroad to other Union troops. Then they killed the Caldwells' milk cows and ate the meat themselves. As a final act of vengeance, they tossed the carcasses into the well to contaminate the water.

Still, the Caldwells continued to hide, nurse, and bury Confederate soldiers who sought refuge at Octagon Hall. The family tried to identify the dead soldiers and notify their next of kin, making arrangements to send the bodies home or bury them on the grounds. It was an arduous task, and many of the soldiers ended up in unmarked or mass graves. Gaunt says their final resting places remain intentionally unmarked today to thwart grave robbers from digging for artifacts.

Dying far from home and being forgotten could upset any spirit wandering the premises, perhaps explaining why one might pick a fight with someone it mistakenly deems responsible for his plight—like Gaunt. He had a frightening encounter with a full-bodied apparition in the house. He came upon a Confederate soldier wearing a white button-down shirt with no collar. Half the soldier's face had been destroyed, and a terrible smell emanated from the ghost. The spirit tried to choke the burly Gaunt, who managed to break free and flee out the door. More mild-mannered spirit soldiers have been mistaken for Civil War reenactors. One was seen walking into the summer kitchen before disappearing, Gaunt says.

Many historic houses have family graveyards on the property, which was a tradition in the late eighteenth and early nineteenth centuries. For example, at Frankfort's Liberty Hall, the Brown family buried relatives near the garden. The Browns' aunt, Mrs. Varick, is the kindly Gray Lady who wanders the hall, but she is the exception. Most former occupants of similar homes stay quietly resting in their graves, causing no mischievous mayhem.

By contrast, the revenants at Octagon Hall roam the halls and stairways and have been seen peering out the wide windows. In fact, because of such frequent activity, paranormal groups routinely rent the home for overnight ghost hunts, which have become a thriving business nationwide. In addition to the Confederate soldiers who died there, the grounds of Octagon Hall became the final resting place for a few Union soldiers who died while occupying the site after the Confederates left, as well as members of the Caldwell family. And not all the spirits reported at Octagon Hall are soldiers. The Caldwells lost two of their eleven children in tragic accidents. Andrew Jackson Jr. was just eighteen months old when he fell down some stairs and broke his neck. In 1851 seven-year-old Mary was standing near the fireplace in the winter kitchen when her clothing caught fire. She died several agonizing days later. One paranormal investigator reported that a spirit child gently held on to the investigator's arm before letting go and leaving. The museum's former director, the late Billy Bird, once saw a young girl standing alone in the basement and asked if he could help her. She just "poofed into black dust."[7]

Literature on Octagon Hall indicates that ancient Native American burial mounds might be present on the property as well. This idea recurs so often in popular fiction and cinema that it's almost a cliché. For example, a haunted house in Amityville, New York—scene of Jay Anson's 1977 book *Amityville Horror* and the movies based on it—was erroneously said to stand on the site of an ancient Native "enclosure for the sick, mad, and dying."[8] Stephen King has used the idea a few times, and several TV horror shows have employed the concept as a backstory. Are we seriously seeing Native American spirits everywhere, or are we just haunted by the massive injustice done to the nation's aboriginal people?

As mysterious as supernatural entities are, Gaunt points out that they require energy from some source to manifest. Simpson County is in the heart of western Kentucky's cave country, with underground rivers and limestone aquifers underlying the entire region. Gaunt suggests that the unseen water moving below our feet might be providing some of the energy the spirits use to appear to us. Also, on many nights, Octagon Hall is inhabited by teams of ghost hunters equipped with fully charged battery packs on their cameras, ghost boxes, and electromagnetic field meters. So there would be plenty of energy available for even the most anemic ghost to show itself.

Ghost hunters often suggest that intense suffering is somehow imprinted into a structure's stones or bricks, resulting in an endless replay that manifests as "residual hauntings"—an idea made popular by anthropologist T. C. Lethbridge in 1961.[9] Although we didn't witness any apparitions during our visit, we believe Octagon Hall has all the requisite elements, including the real-life suffering of the family, the soldiers, and the enslaved people who lived and died on the property. Southern passions and Confederate relics are carefully preserved in a structure built by enslaved workers. Stories of wartime brutality are repeated daily. Revenants or no revenants, we are figuratively haunted by ghosts of the Confederacy, by the mythos of the Lost Cause, and by the belief that supporting an armed rebellion against the legitimate US government was a good idea. By contrast, the ghost-hunting teams that visit Octagon Hall believe they have evidence of literal hauntings—measurable energy, numerous photos, and recordings of electronic voice phenomena. But it's hard to say whether all this is tangible evidence of wraiths or just technological artifacts created by the hunters' modern-day equipment.

For fun, let's add some new possibilities to the mix. Barry Gaunt claims that apparitions aren't the only oddities seen at Octagon Hall. Other weird occurrences include sightings of cryptids and UFOs. People have also visited the property to dowse for ley lines, which were discovered (or invented) by British photographer Alfred Watkins in 1921. They are said to be invisible lines of power connecting spiritual sites across the planet.[10]

It's also possible that some type of unknown energy is responsible for the strange occurrences in and around Octagon Hall. Researchers at Utah's Skinwalker Ranch, for example, believe that the geology of that site may contribute to the multitude of paranormal reports there.[11] Specifically, chemicals given off by volcanic off-gassing may cause witnesses to hallucinate—which would explain the many and varied sightings at the ranch. Western Kentucky's geology is porous but not volcanic, making volcanic off-gassing unlikely, but could human-made toxic chemicals be seeping through the region's underground caves and limestone aquifers? According to the Kentucky Division of Water's website, because of its unique geology, "Simpson County has areas of high sensitivity to groundwater pollution."[12] However, the main groundwater contaminants in the region are agricultural chemicals and soil salts—nothing that heads the list of hallucinogenic substances. So it's unclear what might create a supernatural nexus at one particular location. Why is Octagon Hall a ghost hub—a portal, if you will—and not the historic house down the road that's subject to the same geological conditions?

Lynne Hume, in her 2007 book *Portals*, suggests that at particular times, certain people may experience an "ontic shift," a change in consciousness that makes them feel like "they are no longer dealing with the world as it is known ordinarily, and that this new state is highly significant."[13] This shift may be psychological rather than physical—with brain waves altered mentally, not by chemicals or anything paranormal. Vivid storytelling, for example, can create the sense of an altered, highly significant mental state. The liturgy of a religious service can produce an impression of "holy space" as opposed to "ordinary space." Visiting a historically significant place can also trigger a feeling of astonishment and otherness. When Mason's family vacationed at Cape Canaveral years ago, a wave of amazement washed over him as he stood next to NASA's Vehicle Assembly Building near Launch Pads 39A and 39B.

Octagon Hall's odd shape may help spark an ontic shift. An unusual building draws people's attention and arouses their curiosity about its purpose. Andrew Jackson Caldwell's Masonic symbolism built into the structure's architecture would have puzzled the general public, who might have developed their own explanations for its peculiar appearance. For example, as Colin Dickey argues in *Ghostland*, "The notion of round buildings being built to prevent the Devil from catching you in a corner has a long heritage . . . and it was used sometimes to account for the curious designs of barns used by Quakers and Shakers."[14] Octagon Hall is not round; in fact, it has twice as many corners as a normal building, so this particular folktale motif doesn't apply. Or does it? The Devil would be twice as likely to catch you in a house with twice as many corners.

The Caldwell family had largely died out by the early twentieth century. In 1918 Dr. Miles Williams, an osteopath from Nashville, bought Octagon Hall and lived there until his death in 1954. His heirs rented out the property until 2001, when the Octagon Hall Foundation obtained the building to restore and preserve it. The renters found that the spirits weren't very cooperative roommates. In fact, they could be quite troublesome. According to Gaunt, they would run around upstairs, knock things over, and scream all night long, creating less than ideal living conditions. Not surprisingly, the average renter stayed only two weeks. The longest anyone lived there was four years.

Despite his one unpleasant encounter with a spirit, Gaunt says he's on pretty good terms with most of the other ghosts. He understands their unfortunate plight and speaks to them respectfully, greeting them by saying, "Hello, how's it going?" and identifying himself as their caretaker. He's heard a variety of responses, including an equally friendly "Hello," a desperate "Help me," and a threatening "Get out." But given his nearly fifty-year association with Octagon Hall, it looks as if Gaunt, like the ghosts, is there to stay.

MARY TODD LINCOLN SEEKS SOLACE IN SÉANCES

Curators at the Mary Todd Lincoln House in downtown Lexington tell visitors that the house has never exhibited any evidence of haunting. We politely asked the docents this question several times in different ways, but we always got the same emphatic answer: not haunted—not then, not now, not ever.

Actually, the absence of wraiths at the house on West Main Street in the shadow of Rupp Arena makes sense, since the Todds didn't move there until Mary was fourteen, and she and Abe seldom visited after they were married. However, there are plenty of family artifacts, portraits, and furniture in the fourteen-room house.

Although her family home isn't haunted, the former First Lady certainly was. She was emotionally traumatized by personal losses that would have caused even the most stable person to lose perspective about whether events were real or imaginary. We're not saying that Mary Todd Lincoln lost her mind, although later in life her eldest son committed her to a mental hospital for a brief time. However, in desperation, she embraced the spiritualist craze that swept the nation after the Civil War and was victimized by several brazen con men who took advantage of her fragile mental condition to enrich themselves.

Given the staggering death toll of the Civil War, many families frantically sought one last conversation with a relative killed in combat or a loved one who had died of disease. These families would do anything, believe anything, and pay anything to make that happen. This created a toxic atmosphere that gave rise to charlatans who found fertile ground for various spiritualist hoaxes that deceived these tormented families.

Although Mary didn't lose a son in combat, she suffered other significant losses and, like many others of her time, sought solace from mediums. She had lost her mother by age six. In 1850 the Lincolns' second son, Eddie, died of tuberculosis before his fourth birthday. Then, after barely a year in the White House, the Lincolns' third son, eleven-year-old Willie, died of typhoid fever in February 1862. According to the White House Historical Association:

> First Lady Mary Todd Lincoln became inconsolable after the passing of Willie and desperately searched for an outlet for her grief. Shortly after his death, she was introduced to the Lauries, a well-known group of mediums who were located in Georgetown [a neighborhood in Washington, DC]. Mrs. Lincoln found such comfort from the seances held by the group that she started hosting her own seances in the Red Room of the White House. There is evidence to suggest that she hosted as many as eight seances in the White House and that her husband was even in attendance for a few of them.[1]

Growing up in Lexington, and having a father who was successful in business and politics, Mary Todd Lincoln was "sophisticated, educated, and versed in politics."[2] She held strong opinions and voiced them to her husband when he became the country's sixteenth president, including who he should appoint to certain offices. Mary also understood the hardships of war. She accompanied her husband on visits to army camps and spoke personally with the soldiers, and she volunteered at a Union hospital to minister to wounded soldiers. She watched helplessly as war-related stress aged her husband. Given her background, one wouldn't expect Mary to be easily fooled by con men promising to connect her with her dead sons.[3] Spiritualism, however, was an "international fad" during this period, according to Civil War scholar Ernest B. Furguson. "This was not a superstition restricted to slave and servants; prominent Boston intellectuals, European royalty," and hardheaded men sought mediums "who claimed the magic touch."[4]

Despite being a gracious hostess who entertained influential visitors at the White House, Mary had few friends in Washington. High society was suspicious of her because of the Todd family's loyalties. Six of Mary's siblings supported the Union, while the other eight favored the South either "through marriage or military service."[5] One half-brother allegedly mistreated Union prisoners of war, and a half-sister smuggled goods from the North to the South.

Even though these connections sparked rumors about her alleged Southern sympathies, Mary let some of these family members stay at the White House.

Given her tenuous social standing and her vulnerability, it's understandable that Mary might be influenced by those who flattered her.[6] The spiritualists recognized a cash cow when they saw one, and they milked it for all it was worth. They told a distraught Mary exactly what she wanted to hear—that they could contact the sons she had lost, especially the recently deceased Willie.

Willie and his younger brother, Tad, had been inseparable. But they were a handful and got into mischief wherever they went. In 2008 we wrote a Newspaper in Education series titled "The Lincoln Boys' Adventures," which included searching for secret passageways in the White House, riding a pony through the halls, playing war games with their soldier doll, interrupting presidential meetings, and charging visitors a fee to see their dad. While the staff didn't always appreciate these pranks, the Lincolns indulged their sons and enjoyed the laughter they evoked at such a somber time in history. It was especially devastating for the family to lose Willie when there was already so much sorrow surrounding the war. Mary took to her bed for three weeks and missed Willie's funeral.

The president coped in his own way. Unlike his wife, Lincoln did not believe in spiritualism. According to his longtime friend Ward Hill Lamon, Lincoln "was no dabbler in divination, astrology, horoscopy, prophecy, ghostly lore, or witches of any sort." He put his faith in God. But even so, Lincoln might find it hard to understand why a merciful God would call his two young sons home to heaven so soon. When Willie died, Lincoln didn't consult a medium. He talked directly to his son, without a go-between. "I catch myself every day involuntarily talking with him as if he were with me," Lincoln confessed to a trusted military officer.[7]

Willie died on a Thursday. For several Thursdays after that, Lincoln withdrew to the Green Room to grieve. This worried Mary, and she asked the Reverend Francis Vinton of Trinity Church in New York City for help. Vinton's advice: "Seek not your son among the dead. He is not there. He lives today in Paradise." Whether because of Vinton's words or the fact that the country needed his leadership, Lincoln snapped out of his grief. After placing "a broad black ribbon around his trademark stovepipe hat in Willie's memory," the president moved on.[8]

Meanwhile, Mary was still struggling with her unbearable grief. She desperately wanted to talk to Willie again, making her an easy target for unscrupulous mediums who promised to deliver Willie's spirit to her. "They told her that Willie was still here—anxious to see her, in fact—and simply waited on the other side of a veil that could be lifted by those with the proper gift."[9]

Our only attempt to contact the Great Beyond was performed by Mason and his sister, Martha, when they were children. Someone gave them a Ouija board for Christmas, and their only session with the oracle resulted in the planchette spelling out "you are stupid." Mason wants to believe this message was guided by his sister and was not the verdict of the Realms of Darkness.

During a nineteenth-century séance, "People sat hand-in-hand around tables in the dark, to hear bells rung and drums thumped and banjos twanged," according to historian Margaret Leech.[10] It sounds corny to us, but probably not to a despondent mother who craved contact with a beloved son she sorely missed. Mary occasionally used Charles Colchester, a popular young "red-faced, blue-eyed Englishman with a large mustache," as a medium.[11] Followers considered him a "gifted intermediary," while skeptics labeled him a con man "who employed sleight of hand, hypnosis and sideshow magic in darkened rooms to fill his pockets at the expense of the troubled and the brokenhearted."[12] Colchester could reportedly "read sealed letters, cry out the names of visitors' deceased friends, cause apparitions to appear, and produce words on his forearm in blood-red letters."[13] For Mary, he produced scratches and taps that he interpreted as messages from Willie.

Yet it wasn't during a séance that Mary finally heard from Willie. He visited her on his own. In October 1863 Mary confided to her half-sister Emilie Todd Helm, "Willie lives. He comes to me every night and stands at the foot of the bed with the same sweet adorable smile he always has had." Even better, Willie didn't always come alone. "Little Eddie is sometimes with him," she reported, "and twice he has come with our brother, Alex." Mary's brother, twenty-three-year-old Alexander Todd, had been fighting for the South at Baton Rouge in August 1862 when he was injured by friendly fire. Todd died from his wounds two weeks later.[14] Emilie was freaked out by this ghostly visitation, but Mary couldn't have been happier. "It is unnatural and abnormal," Emilie wrote in her diary. "It frightens me." However, the visits consoled the previously inconsolable mother. "You cannot dream of the comfort this gives me," Mary wrote.[15]

Although Lincoln was a nonbeliever, he let Mary hold some of her séances in the White House. He even attended a few, partly to support his grieving wife but also to prevent her from squandering the family's money on charlatans. Lincoln biographer Carl Sandburg believes Lincoln had ulterior motives for attending the séance on April 23, 1863. Joining the Lincolns and medium

Charles E. Shockle were two cabinet secretaries and a *Boston Gazette* reporter. Lincoln answered questions good-naturedly, almost humorously, during the session to show that he was a good sport. According to Sandburg, Lincoln's attendance might have been a "shrewd political ploy" to demonstrate that in the midst of war the commander in chief "could sit back and sample the same kind of parlor-room novelty that other Americans were marveling over."[16] Historians have hypothesized that the session was "a publicity stunt to show the president in a more everyday-man light."[17]

Some nineteenth- and early twentieth-century hoaxers used chemicals to produce smoke or clouds of vapor during séances. "I feel the departed drawing ever nearer!" they'd declare, and suddenly, poof! Smoke would appear. The medium would then explain (while secretly shoving the vapor-producing device back under a chair) that this "mystical vapor" was a manifestation of ectoplasm and that the dearly departed were now present. But ghosts don't consist of vapor. After all, we can see clouds, measure them, and even weigh them. Ghosts are different. There can never be any physical proof of them because they are not physical beings. Ghosts don't leave footprints, although we have collected a few fuzzy photos.

Like many spiritualists of the time, Charles Colchester was proved to be a fraud. He was caught wearing "a specially designed electrical noisemaker strapped to his biceps" and hidden by his clothes. Colchester apparently showed no remorse, claiming that he was "honest if he liked a client" but "often cheated the fools, as he could easily do it." The only legitimate information Colchester ever offered was a warning that Lincoln was in danger of being assassinated. But he didn't glean that information from spirits. It was an inside scoop from none other than John Wilkes Booth himself, whom Colchester knew. Lincoln knew he had political enemies within the divided United States, so the threat was no big surprise. Still, Lincoln mistakenly believed that no one hated him enough to kill him.[18]

Mary's grief was assuaged by Willie's and Eddie's occasional visits, but she still had two living sons to worry about. Tad, who was only nine when Willie died, was too young to join the army, but the Lincolns' oldest son, eighteen-year-old Robert, was willing to serve his country. Mary prevented his enlistment by sending Robert off to college until the waning days of the Civil War, when she finally gave in. But Robert certainly wasn't sent to the front lines, even though the president wanted him to get no special treatment, stressing to Mary, "Our son is not more dear to us than the sons of other people are to their mother."[19] In the final days of the war, starting in January 1865, Robert joined General U. S. Grant's staff as a captain, making it unlikely that he would see combat. Indeed, he didn't, and he survived the war intact.

Just months after Robert's assignment, President Lincoln was assassinated on April 14, 1865, while taking a rare night off to enjoy a play at Ford's Theatre. Mary was seated next to him when he was shot, and she understandably became hysterical. Lincoln was taken to a neighboring boardinghouse, where his wife's wailing, shrieking, and convulsing were so distracting that she was forced to leave. Mary never saw her husband alive again. Still fragile from her other devastating losses, Mary spent forty days in bed crying and moaning; she was unable to attend her husband's funeral. The grieving widow's extended stay also made it awkward for President Andrew Johnson to move into the White House.

Not surprisingly, several self-styled spiritualists rushed to the White House to console Mary, and the greedy opportunists purported to give her posthumous messages from her husband.[20] She needed reassurance that he would somehow return to her—in spirit if not in body. The darkened rooms, the hand-holding, and the theatrics of a séance comforted her.

By May 1865, Mary was heavily in debt and moved to Chicago with her two sons. More tragedy followed six years later when Tad died at age eighteen; his cause of death could have been anything from tuberculosis to pneumonia. Mary fell into a deep depression and began to consult mediums in disguise, using fake names such as Mrs. Linder.

But séance spiritualists weren't the only con artists preying on Mrs. Lincoln. In 1872 Mary, using the alias Mrs. Tindall, commissioned a photograph by spiritualist William Mumler in Boston. Seated, she wore a bulky coat and a fashionable bonnet with ribbons that tied in a big bow under her chin. To her surprise, once the photo was developed, Mary discovered that she wasn't alone. Standing behind Mary was a faint but distinguishable image of her long-dead husband gazing lovingly down at her, with his ghostly hands resting gently on her shoulders. Fact-checking site Snopes.com has this to say about the photo: "Mumler did not magically capture a picture of Lincoln's ghost. The photographer made a living producing manipulated studio photographs with faded figures visible behind his subjects. This was not digital manipulation like we see in modern photography. The idea of doctoring photographs in the 19th century meant trickery in the exposure and development process of glass plate images."[21]

To be fair to Mrs. Lincoln, photography was a relatively new technology in the mid-nineteenth century, and people simply didn't understand how it captured the likenesses of living people, let alone ghostly photo bombers. Mumler sold copies of the controversial photo and was later charged with conspiracy to defraud his customers. But even with expert photographers testifying that Mumler had altered the photos, nothing was ever proved conclusively.

Whether Mary Todd Lincoln acknowledged the fake or not, she continued to spend money she couldn't afford on these hoaxers. So in 1875 her only surviving son, Robert, committed his mother to an asylum in Batavia, Illinois. Her stay was brief, and upon her release, Mary moved to Europe until 1881, when she returned to her sister Elizabeth's home in Illinois. A year after her return to America, Mary died of a stroke at age sixty-three. She is entombed with Lincoln in Oak Ridge Cemetery in Springfield, Illinois.

As far as we know, Mary has not tried to contact anyone after her death. However, Mason believes that, during our tour, he saw one of the chairs in the Mary Todd Lincoln House move on its own. Maybe we should alert the docents.

HAUNTED HISTORIC HOMES AND PLACES

THE HAND ON THE RAILING

The Lion of White Hall Still Roars

The majestic White Hall State Historic Site north of Richmond is one of those places that just *looks* like it should have ghosts haunting its stairways and halls. Sure enough, nearly every tour guide, past and present, has a story about a supernatural encounter with one or more of the house's former residents, including the contentious Cassius Marcellus Clay, a fiery nineteenth-century abolitionist and personal friend of Abraham Lincoln.

During its heyday, the mansion was filled with drama and turmoil among the strong-willed, colorful, and sometimes violent Clay family, so it's not surprising that there might be some troubled spirits hanging around. For example, in his 2001 biography of Clay, Kevin McQueen devotes twenty pages to stories of paranormal activity in the restored mansion.[1] Although McQueen, a former White Hall tour guide himself, never experienced any weird goings-on, many of his colleagues reported full-body apparitions, strange smells, disembodied voices, and the unexplained opening and closing of doors.

Stephanie Thurman, who has worked at White Hall for nearly a decade, told us in a June 2022 interview that guides have seen men, women, and children in nineteenth-century attire appear out of nowhere and then disappear just as quickly. They have smelled what could be Cassius's cigar smoke and his wife Mary Jane's favorite rose-scented perfume. She also mentioned furniture moving on its own, footsteps where no earthly person is treading, and voices coming from empty rooms. Thurman recalls her former supervisor, Kathleen, getting goose bumps when she saw a man's hand gliding down the banister by the back stairs. Above the hand was a white-cuffed shirt and a heavy black sleeve. Kathleen left in a hurry, but she later remembered where she had seen that image before—in a portrait of Clay painted when he was eighty-four.

In the painting, his hand—extending out of a white-cuffed sleeve and black jacket—hangs over the armrest of his chair.

Other witnesses have caught glimpses of Clay, a tall man with dark hair dressed in nineteenth-century garb, standing on the porch or striding across the lawn at night. However, skeptics would argue that these witnesses were conjuring this image from nothing more than a shadow falling across window glass in the deepening twilight.

So, who was this formidable man? Born to wealth in Madison County, Kentucky, in 1810, Clay earned the nickname the Lion of White Hall. As a fearless journalist, politician, emancipationist, and ambassador to Russia, Clay made lots of friends—and enemies. Writing in the *Wall Street Journal* in 2021, Michael Medved noted, "Clay defied his slave-owning and influential Kentucky family when he became an abolitionist during his student days at Yale. A speech by William Lloyd Garrison, the impassioned advocate for emancipation, struck him 'as water to a thirsty wayfarer.'"[2] Once converted, Clay used his family fortune to establish an abolitionist newspaper, the *True American*, in Lexington and to fund Berea College, the first Kentucky institution to welcome Black students.

David and Jeanne Heidler, biographers of the venerable US Senator Henry Clay, wrote of his cousin Cassius: "A venomous pen was his first weapon of choice, a Bowie knife his second, and because he was so effective with the one, he found it wise to have the other handy."[3] A typical example of Clay's fondness for rhetoric and weapons reportedly occurred on Vine Street in downtown Lexington while Clay was giving one of his inflammatory antislavery speeches. He stepped up to the podium with a Bible in one hand and a .45 revolver in the other. "If I can't convince you that slavery is an abomination by the words of our Lord and Savior Jesus Christ," he shouted, brandishing the Bible, "then you can just talk with Colonel Colt!" He emphasized that last point by waving his pistol around in full view of the audience. This story might not be historically accurate, but Clay certainly used his gun and Bowie knife to fight off more than one attacker, and he once deployed two four-pounder brass cannons to discourage a mob trying to destroy his Lexington newspaper office.

Despite his political differences with the family, Clay, the youngest of seven children, inherited Clermont from his wealthy slave-owning father, Green Clay. The original house, a modest two-story brick home built in 1798 on what is now the White Hall site, contained seven rooms that covered roughly three thousand square feet. During the Civil War, while Cassius was serving as the American ambassador to Imperial Russia, his wife and the mother of their ten children, Mary Jane Warfield Clay, oversaw the expansion of their home into the mansion that stands today, with forty-five rooms occupying more than ten thousand square feet.[4]

Although they were married for forty-five years, the Clays separated shortly after Cassius returned from Russia in 1868 with an unexpected guest—a young boy that many believed was his son from an affair with a Russian ballerina. When the Clays divorced in 1878, Cassius kept the house, and Mary Jane and the children moved to Lexington, where she died in 1900.

Meanwhile, Cassius grew more eccentric over the years. In 1894, at age eighty-four, he married fifteen-year-old Dora Richardson but divorced her four years later because she had a boyfriend. However, Dora later served as Clay's housekeeper and caregiver.

Even in his old age, Clay kept a gun handy. While in his eighties, he reportedly killed two men who broke into White Hall, where he was living alone. The would-be robbers didn't expect a fight from their geriatric target. That was a deadly mistake on their part.

After Clay died in 1903, his grandson rented the house to tenant farmers, who damaged it by sheltering barn animals indoors. The mansion stood vacant for a while, making it a prime target for vandals. Finally, Clay's descendants donated the property to the commonwealth of Kentucky in 1968, which renovated the mansion; filled it with the original furnishings, portraits, and possessions of the Clay family; and opened the restored house to the public in 1971. Once part of the Kentucky parks system, it's now managed by Eastern Kentucky University.

Although Stephanie Thurman has had some unsettling experiences with White Hall spirits, such as the time she heard her name being called when no one was around, she has never felt threatened or in danger. She doesn't consider the house to be *haunted* so much as *occupied* by members of the Clay family. "My philosophy about the ghosts is that it's *their* house," she said. "If they don't want to leave, I'm not going to make them. If they want to stay, that's fine. I'm not going to argue with them. But I've tried to make a point with them that I'm here to take care of their things." As she moves through the house each morning, Thurman calls out "Hello!" to announce her presence. Then she describes out loud what she's doing in the room so the spirits won't bother her, having been reassured that she won't damage anything.

It might be helpful to define a few ghost-hunting terms using the expertise of Grant Wilson, one of the founders of TAPS—The Atlantic Paranormal

Society—for the TV series *Ghost Hunters.* Wilson says restless spirits fall into three categories: specters, poltergeists, and elementals.

Specters, also called residual hauntings, are floating apparitions that tend to manifest on stairways and appear to glide silently across a room—unaware of or undeterred by the presence of living researchers shouting questions at them like persistent members of the White House press corps. According to Wilson, specters are like flashbulb afterimages and are considered harmless.

Poltergeists (German for "noisy ghosts") seem to be aware of the humans sharing their environment. They can physically move things and occasionally impart messages. The ghost of Hamlet's father is a poltergeist. He manifests visually and tells Hamlet, "I was murdered by your Uncle Claudius, and now it's your job to avenge me, so hop to it," or words to that effect. Poltergeists are the most bothersome kind of spirits, and the TAPS team often encourages such wraiths to move toward the light, which might have been a better approach for Hamlet rather than killing everybody in his orbit.

Elementals are swirling masses of darkness that have never been human. The TAPS team considers elementals too hot to handle. They usually call a priest to exorcise these evil spirits, sending them elsewhere.[5] The word *elemental* has been around since biblical times. It shows up in two letters of St. Paul (depending on the translation)—in Colossians 2:8 and Galatians 4:3, where Paul references the forces of cosmic evil in the universe. Other ancient writers see elemental spirits as more benevolent—earthly spirits of Air, Water, Fire, and Earth that guard the cosmos.

Unfortunately, some of this ghost-hunting terminology—phrases such as *residual energy*, *spiritual vibrations*, and *ethereal realms*—seems suspiciously divorced from any kind of physical referent. For example, how many volts, ohms, or watts of residual energy does a specter emit? And where does this energy reside? If residual energy was originally generated by a complex life-form, how is it stored or transmitted once that life-form is gone?

The architecture of White Hall, both the original Clermont and Mary Jane's additions, might play a part in housing ghosts. The main stairways of the much larger White Hall mansion lead to the three aboveground floors, while smaller staircases lead to different levels of the same "floor."

Carolyn L. Siegel, who worked as a White Hall guide in the 1980s and wrote *Cassius Marcellus Clay: The Man Behind the Legend*, told us that on inclement summer afternoons she would sometimes drive to the house before the thunderstorm struck. She liked how the many gables and odd-shaped corners made the house whistle and groan like a ship at sea.

Some of the modern conveniences Cassius and Mary Jane installed, which were revolutionary at the time, may also contribute to the hauntings. They had a system that allowed for the flushing of toilets decades before indoor plumbing became the norm. Rainwater from the roof was directed into a large reservoir between the second and third floors. The stored water could then flow to a tub and toilet. Siegel says that rainwater gushing into the reservoir made creepy noises. Not surprisingly, a number of the paranormal incidents reported in McQueen's book occurred during storms and happened around the hot spot near the water reservoir.

Other theories that seek to explain ghostly sightings range from simple hallucinations or a runaway imagination to lengthy descriptions that claim witnesses are experiencing the imprint of psychic energy on the environment—in other words, the energy of those who once lived there can still be sensed today. If none of these possibilities seem plausible, know that even professional ghost hunters can be stumped. "There *is* something out there, and we don't know what it is," says Elaine Davison, a paranormal investigator from Oregon. "But I will tell you that most of it is bad wiring."[6]

Before becoming a ghost hunter, Grant Wilson worked as a plumber for Roto-Rooter. That experience has come in handy in his second career. Wilson and his partners at TAPS often discover that the mysterious noises in a client's basement come from defective pipes, not from lost souls trapped in this spiritual plane. So, if one takes into account weird shadows, flawed plumbing, and faulty wiring, it's easy to debunk almost any ghost story. But there are other concerns beyond physical issues that should be considered before we summarily dismiss all eyewitness accounts. There could be historical and emotional reasons why people see certain ghosts.

Carolyn Siegel said she never felt comfortable in White Hall's basement and refused to go down there alone. Employees clocked in at a station near the back stairs, and Siegel would wait for others to arrive before venturing downstairs. Kevin McQueen shares a typical White Hall ghost story about the bewildering basement. This one includes Siegel as a witness:

> She and two other guides were relaxing in the powder room, there having been no 4:30 tour that day. Suddenly they became aware of muffled voices rising from the vents, revealing a conversation of some sort taking place in the basement. The guides, aware that they were supposed to be the only

> people in the house, decided to set a trap for the speakers. Brandishing the only weapons handy—a carving knife, a serving fork, and a large metal hook—they went to different entrances to the basement, ensuring that no intruders could escape undetected. The voices ceased, and the intrepid guides found no human conversationalists.[7]

Apparently, in addition to being a successful lawyer, landowner, banker, distiller, ferry operator, and general in the Kentucky militia, Cassius's father was a justice of the peace for many years. Any prisoners who had to be held until the sheriff could come and collect them were chained in a dark corner of the low-ceilinged, claustrophobic basement room. No wonder the basement makes guides and guests feel uneasy.

In his book *Ghostland*, Colin Dickey argues that many American "ghosts" aren't see-through wraiths made of ectoplasm but unresolved historical memories. Dickey cites the example of Chloe, an enslaved woman whose ghost is said to inhabit the Myrtles Plantation in Louisiana. Her lurid story includes being sexually exploited by her master and having her ears cut off when she was caught eavesdropping on the family. Chloe then either deliberately or accidentally poisoned the family by putting oleander leaves in a cake she served them. She might have been seeking revenge, or perhaps she wanted to be the hero who healed the family and just misjudged how much oleander would make them sick but not kill them. Either way, the wife and a couple of the children reportedly died, so other enslaved people hanged Chloe and tossed her body into the Mississippi River. Although there is no historical record of this story, tourists are told the tale of Chloe's brutal treatment and tragic death.

Millions of enslaved people lived and died in the pre–Civil War South, and few, if any, received justice for the barbarous conditions they endured. In sharing stories about women like Chloe, we're attempting to grant them justice and peace in the present, according to Dickey. "Ghost stories are about how we face, or fail to face, the past—how we process information, how we narrate our past, and how we make sense of the gaps in that history," he writes.[8]

Think about how many ghost stories start with an injustice: the murdered lover, the desecrated burial ground, the untimely death, perhaps in battle. We can't go back in time to right these wrongs, but perhaps telling stories of revenge beyond the grave provides these characters some narrative justice. According to Dickey: "If you listen closely, the ghost stories of the Myrtles Plantation say more about the tellers than they do about the supernatural. A slave abused by her master, who in response turns murderous; the Indian ghosts whose burial lands have been disturbed—all of these stories, in one way or another, respond to history."[9]

The three generations of Clays who lived at White Hall experienced—or in many cases created—plenty of injustice and unhappiness. Think of the prisoners confined in the basement, anxiously awaiting their punishment. Think of the men Cassius killed over political disagreements. Then there was Cassius and Mary Jane's unhappy marriage, which ended in divorce, and finally, the elderly Clay's years alone in that massive house. That's a lot of history, a lot of emotional baggage, and a lot of restless souls.

Humans need a frame of reference to describe such deep and disturbing psychological experiences. Dickey calls this our "symbolic matrix." During medieval times, society's symbolic matrix included a spiritual world that easily incorporated ghosts, monsters, and other mysterious things that go bump in the night—and it included sure and severe justice beyond death for those who failed to get justice in life. Dickey argues that modern humans long for those romantic days when the world was enchanted and people routinely encountered strange creatures in the woods, ghosts on the staircase, or angels in the skies.[10] But there may be more to this yearning than simple romanticism because people are still encountering anomalous things in all those places—things that are not standard, normal, or expected.

It's easy to dismiss ghost reports as the imagination running amok, pranks gone awry, or the weird sound and light effects of unusual architecture. White Hall, however, has a history of sightings going back decades. Many people, not all of them believers in the supernatural, have reported strange things happening at that mansion.

Although she is on pretty good terms with the spirits, Stephanie Thurman says they can push her buttons, like the time the candles in all the rooms fell out of their candleholders at the same time and scattered across the floor. But that spectral prank seemed more mischievous than evil. Still, Thurman told the spunky spirits quite sternly that she didn't appreciate the extra work and to cut it out. The stunt has never been repeated. While she had their attention, Thurman set down some other ground rules. "I told them that I don't want anyone to touch me, and I don't want anyone to jump out at me." The "residents" of White Hall have been honoring these rules as well.

So perhaps the ghosts will be on their best behavior when you visit.

THE GRAY LADY

The Helpful Spirit at Liberty Hall

We eyed the dark clouds rolling in as we parked in front of Liberty Hall in Frankfort. Our tour of this historic house on Wilkinson Street wouldn't start for another fifteen minutes, but afternoon thunderstorms were expected, and a few raindrops were already falling on the windshield. The stormy forecast seemed right for our visit. We were particularly interested in the hall's most famous ghost: a specter photographed in 1965 ascending (or perhaps descending) the long stairway. The apparition's image is vague.

Liberty Hall, home of the John Brown family and their descendants for four generations, apparently still houses this spirit known as the Gray Lady, the beloved aunt of Mrs. Brown. The Gray Lady's image strongly resembles an even more prominent photograph of the Brown Lady (no relation to the Kentucky Browns) taken at Raynham Hall in Norfolk, England, in 1936. That apparition, which is also ascending or descending a long stairway, is supposed to be the restless spirit of Lady Townsend, murdered by her husband for infidelity.[1] Both women were assigned their nicknames based on the color scheme of the clothing they were last seen wearing.

We wanted to see the setting of the Gray Lady's famous photo for ourselves. Luckily, tour guide Debra Parrish invited us in just as the gentle drizzle turned into a downpour. We got only sightly damp before heavy rain pounded the roof and swept over the street like a wave hitting the beach.

Since we were the only ones who had braved the weather, we got a private tour, which started at the foot of that well-known staircase. But the storm wasn't through wreaking havoc and setting the perfect stage for a spirited encounter. The lights blinked off and on once, twice, three times. Thunder accompanied the guide's narrative about the house's history. It was an ominous start to the supernatural tale tied to the Browns' story.

Despite the stormy backdrop, the Gray Lady did not appear during our tour, neither on the staircase nor in the upstairs bedroom where she died in 1817. Granted, we weren't expecting her to welcome us at the door or ask to take our umbrella or mop up the raindrops dripping from our damp clothes, even though witnesses claim she's a kind-hearted spirit who's always willing to lend a helping hand to others. Besides, it was 11:00 a.m., and the most productive high-tech ghost-hunting expeditions tend to be launched in the middle of the night. Liberty Hall, however, isn't open at 2:00 a.m., which is known as the "haunting hour," when spirits are thought to be most active. It was just as well, since that's not prime time for us either.

While staying alert for signs of the genial ghost, we learned that Liberty Hall was originally the home of John Brown (1757–1837), who started his thirty-year political career as a member of the Continental Congress from Virginia. He was later elected one of Kentucky's first two US senators. In fact, Brown's work and his political connections helped Kentucky achieve statehood in 1792.[2]

Brown built Liberty Hall in 1796 using plans designed by none other than Thomas Jefferson, a fellow Virginian with whom Brown had studied law. The mansion sat on four acres near the Kentucky River in what was then a rustic frontier town, population 628.[3] The house was (and still is) magnificent, but living in Frankfort must have been quite an adjustment for Brown's new wife, Margaretta Mason, whom he married in 1799. Mrs. Brown, a well-educated, independent, and resourceful woman with her own political and religious views, left New York and moved to Kentucky in 1801. She added a few personal touches to the mansion, such as antiques, mirrors, brass door handles, and silk fabrics, to spruce things up.

Most of the furniture and household goods displayed in the home are originals, since the house stayed in the family for 130 years. It was willed to the Colonial Dames of America in 1956 and opened as a museum. Although Liberty Hall's purpose is to "create an interest in history and stimulate a spirit of patriotism," our guide humored us by answering questions about ghosts.[4]

Living in a small Kentucky town off the beaten path (in fact, off the buffalo trails that initially served as highways) didn't deter the Browns from socializing with a Who's Who of the time. They hosted parties for various dignitaries, and the 1819 guest list included President James Monroe, Colonel Zachary Taylor, Colonel Andrew Jackson, and French General Lafayette. The generous family also opened their home to neighbors for weddings and funerals.

Life wasn't a cakewalk for the Browns, though. Like many frontier families, they suffered their share of setbacks and heartbreaks. The couple had five children, but only two sons lived to adulthood. Mason Brown later inherited his childhood home, and his younger brother Orlando lived in another mansion next door. Debra Parrish told us that the Browns' other two sons died in infancy, and their only daughter, Euphemia, passed away from typhoid fever at age seven, all in a ten-year span (1804–1814). Those losses were too much for Mrs. Brown to bear, and she fell into a deep depression. She asked her aunt Margaretta Varick to come and stay with the family.

The two women shared the same first name, and in fact, Mrs. Varick had raised Mrs. Brown after her own mother died. Being a compassionate soul, the sixty-five-year-old Mrs. Varick made the long, strenuous journey by coach and horseback to help her niece deal with her grief. The already frail woman arrived in Frankfort completely worn out from her travels. Three days later, on July 28, 1817, she died in an upstairs bedroom from a heart attack, acute indigestion, or exhaustion.[5] The distraught Browns buried Mrs. Varick in the small family cemetery located in the backyard garden. But because they didn't place a headstone on the grave, the exact location is unknown. Thus, when other family members buried in the same graveyard were moved and reinterred in the much larger Frankfort Cemetery in the late 1840s, Mrs. Varick was left behind—abandoned by the family she loved.

This abandonment might be reason enough for even a good-natured ghost to haunt her relatives' home, at least until someone remembers where they buried her, exhumes her body, and reunites her with the rest of the family. But by all accounts, Mrs. Varick isn't a vindictive specter. Witnesses who have seen her in the upstairs bedroom or felt her presence elsewhere in the house say she is a caring spirit who just wants to be useful as she whiles away the endless hours. She has been known to do chores such as folding blankets or mending clothes, as well as opening gates and shutting doors for people. In the 1980s volunteer curator Eugenia Blackburn, who lived in a separate apartment at Liberty Hall, discovered that the kindly wraith had washed the windows and dusted the tables for her. Some overnight guests have reported that a smiling female apparition tried to tuck them in at night.[6]

If this gentle ghost ever gets tired of haunting her Frankfort home, we could use a hand with our housework in Richmond. She comes with great references. However, it's unlikely that we could convince Mrs. Varick to move. She seems pretty attached to Liberty Hall, making her first ghostly appearance a few years after she died. She then stepped up her game after the other family members' graves were moved. Family, staff, and visitors have reported seeing an older woman wearing a gray house dress (thus her epithet the Gray Lady) in nearly every room in the mansion, especially in Mrs. Varick's upstairs bedroom and on the main staircase.[7]

Liberty Hall's website mentions that in one of her first surprise spiritual visits, the Gray Lady startled the new bride of Benjamin Gatz Brown, Senator Brown's grandson. The couple was staying in Mrs. Varick's old bedroom. Happy honeymoon, and welcome to the family!

But Mrs. Varick visited Benjamin's niece Mary Mason Scott most often. Maybe that's because Mary resembled Mrs. Varick and slept in the bedroom where she died. Mary woke up one night to find a "tall woman veiled in gray" standing next to her bed. Scared by the unexpected apparition, Mary screamed, which brought her brother, John Matthew, to the rescue, armed with a loaded shotgun. The ghost disappeared in all the commotion.[8]

Apparently, the apparition didn't take the hint that her nocturnal visits were upsetting Mary, because the Gray Lady came calling three nights in a row. Finally, realizing there was no threat, Mary began to refer to the apparition as "our beloved ghost." In the 1920s, Mary was the last of the Brown family to live in the mansion, and Mrs. Varick tried to use Mary to guide others to her unmarked grave. Unfortunately, that effort was unsuccessful, but it's possible the Gray Lady is still trying to direct mortals to her final resting place on the grounds of Liberty Hall.

There have been many other Gray Lady sightings over the years. Witnesses report seeing her staring out of an upstairs window, wandering in the garden, or, of course, standing on the front staircase where her image was captured.

Volunteer curator Frances Coleman took a series of pictures to document the restoration of the house after a 1965 fire. There was no other living person around at the time, but when Coleman developed the film, one image showed a "vaporous figure on the stairs" that looked a lot like the Gray Lady.[9]

Debra Parrish mentioned that motorists driving by at night often see an "aura-type thing" emanating from the mansion. But she has never experienced any ghostly activity while giving tours of the hall. Parrish also shared a story about an employee who brought his young son to work with him one day. The child was sent upstairs to play, and the father occasionally heard him talking to someone. At quitting time, he asked the boy who his playmate had been. He responded, "The nice old lady who lives here." No living person resided in the house, and Parrish says the child was too young to invent such a story.

Mrs. Varick might not be the only ghost haunting Liberty Hall. A Spanish opera singer was a guest at the mansion in 1805. During a party in her honor, she went for a solitary walk in the garden and headed toward the Kentucky River, unaware of the dangers lurking in the wilderness. She never returned.[10] Officials dragged the river but found no body. Theories about her disappearance include that she was "abducted by either Native Americans or despicable characters who were attracted by the lights and the noise of the party." Over the years, "a dark-haired female apparition with her mouth frozen open in a soundless cry of terror has been seen running frantically through [the] garden on hot, humid nights."[11] Perhaps the woman is still performing her final oratorio, as some witnesses claim that, at times, "you can hear the soprano voice of an opera singer in the gardens."[12] All we heard during our visit, besides our guide's voice, was thunder and the occasional car passing by on rain-soaked Wilkinson Street.

Unlike other haunted venues in Kentucky, Liberty Hall was well maintained by a single family into the twentieth century, and its outside features don't scream "haunted" or appear to be somewhere Morticia and Gomez Addams might live. In contrast, White Hall near Richmond and Octagon Hall near Bowling Green have enough unusual architectural features to make them look a bit odd, eccentric, or "ghostly." Even after being restored following some difficult years of disrepair or damage, these historic homes still seem more "hauntable" than others.

Paranormal author Hans Holzer (1920–2009) spent his lifetime collecting information and writing about the supernatural. His book *Ghosts: True Encounters with the World Beyond* suggests that "exceptional circumstances" are needed for a person's spirit to remain earthbound after death. In his chapter "What Every Would-be Ghost Hunter Should Know," Holzer says that, contrary to popular belief, ghosts are not dangerous and do not hurt people:

> Nor are ghosts figments of the imagination, or the product of motion picture writers. Ghostly experiences are neither supernatural nor unnatural; they fit into the general pattern of the universe we live in, although the majority of conventional scientists don't yet understand what exactly ghosts are. Some do, however. Those who have studied parapsychology have come to understand that human life does continue beyond what we commonly call death. Once in a while, there are extraordinary circumstances surrounding a death, and these exceptional circumstances create what we popularly call ghosts and haunted houses.[13]

At Liberty Hall, the extraordinary circumstances might include Mrs. Varick's unexpected death and the fact that her grave site is unknown.

Holzer does not necessarily deserve to have the final word on the subject of ghostly motivations. His long list of paranormal publications includes two absurdly credulous books about a New York case that turned out to be a gigantic hoax: the Amityville haunting in Long Island. He also published two books, *Elvis Presley Speaks* (1979) and *Elvis Speaks from Beyond* (1993), that won't win any prizes for scientific rigor. So although we cite Holzer, we recognize that his evaluation of the evidence might not be as careful as one would hope.

Skeptics would say that sightings of the Gray Lady amount to nothing more than spooky stories and a blurry picture. Even believers would point out that she doesn't seem to be unhappy, tortured, or lost. She just got tired of traveling and decided to stay a while—a *long* while. This ghost is the friendly variety—like the cartoon ghost Casper. No one has been injured or threatened by the Gray Lady, so there's no compelling reason to bring in archaeologists and hire ground-penetrating radar to locate and move Mrs. Varick's grave—which might have been washed away in the Kentucky River years ago.

Although we didn't see her spirit during our visit, if you tour Liberty Hall and happen to pass a semitransparent Mrs. Varick on the stairs, don't be a screamer like Jamie Lee Curtis in the *Halloween* movies. Instead, be like Elwood P. Dowd, the main character in Mary Chase's 1944 screenplay *Harvey*. Elwood is best friends with a giant white rabbit named Harvey that no one else can see. When Elwood first met Harvey, he didn't react with fear, and he certainly didn't scream. Elwood describes their first encounter: "Well, anyway, I was walking down along the street and I heard this voice saying, 'Good evening, Mr. Dowd.' Well, I turned around and here was this big six-foot rabbit leaning up against a lamp-post. Well, I thought nothing of that because when you've lived in a town as long as I've lived in this one, you get used to the fact that everybody knows your name. And naturally I went over to chat with him."[14]

Be like Elwood. Go over and chat. Mrs. Varick is a gentle, helpful ghost. And if you're worried about having nothing to say to a person who's been dead since 1817, you could start with, "Good afternoon, Mrs. Varick. You've certainly kept your family's house looking lovely for the past two hundred years. How do you manage it?"

STILL HANGING AROUND

Jesse James, the Blue Lady, and Uncle Fred

We sat crowded together with other ghost tour enthusiasts in a dimly lit upstairs room of the Old Talbott Tavern in Bardstown—phones charged, camera function open, and eyes peeled. We were hoping to digitally capture an apparition lurking in a dark corner. Specifically, we were hunting ghost orbs—small colored balls of light that are believed to be a ghost's way of showing itself to the living.

On a cue from paranormal researcher Patti Starr, we started snapping away at everything in our viewfinders, whether it looked spooky or not. Few witnesses notice these elusive orbs with the naked eye, but orbs sometimes appear faintly in photos when sensitive cameras are aimed at notably haunted areas. Ghost hunters claim that highly pixilated still cameras can record minute amounts of energy—perhaps spiritual energy—that the eye alone can't detect. Orbs are occasionally discovered on videos flitting around like a swarm of fireflies, clearly visible in the image once it's replayed but apparently invisible to the humans in the room when it was originally shot.

Ghost orbs are likely artifacts of the digital cameras themselves—tiny amounts of light reflected from dust motes triggering the pixels to fire. At least, that's what the skeptics argue. But if you're in the famously haunted Old Talbott Tavern late at night with a genuine ghost hunter, that sounds like crazy talk. Our group of believers was primed to capture something supernatural, and given the number of frames we shot with and without flash, we were disappointed to find that the spirits had eluded us all.

This didn't deter Patti Starr, who shared more ghost stories, along with Bardstown history, as we continued our tour into the nearby Pioneer Cemetery. We shot plenty of photos there too, but the orbs were not with us on that cool fall night. Patti struggled to be heard over more earthly sounds—loud country-western music spilling out of a nearby pub and cars and trucks rumbling in the downtown area on a busy weekend night. So that might have scared off these otherwise frisky specters.

Interestingly, the most famous spirit spotted at Talbott Tavern is also the first person who claimed to have seen a ghost at the popular stagecoach stop. The legendary outlaw Jesse James (1847–1882) frequented the tavern during his lifetime—and reportedly still visits after being murdered. The thirty-four-year-old James was gunned down in his own home in Saint Joseph, Missouri, by a new member of his gang of bank, train, and stagecoach robbers hoping to collect the $5,000 reward.[1] James has shown up in photographs taken by "walkers" like us who followed Patti around the tavern, outside the jail, and into the nearby graveyard.

While James was still among the living, he would hang out with his cousin Donnie Pence, who was, ironically, the Nelson County sheriff. The sheriff's office and jail (also said to be haunted) was conveniently located next door to the tavern. James had a taste for Kentucky bourbon, and travel journalist Jenn Shockley reports that after a night of heavy drinking, James thought he saw someone in his private room at the tavern, so he grabbed his gun and fired repeatedly.[2] But whoever or whatever he had seen had disappeared by then—simply vanished. If the shadow James shot at was human, he apparently wasn't hit—there was no blood and no body. And even drunk, James was not the sort of marksman to miss at point-blank range. Despite damage to the tavern from a 1998 fire, the bullet holes in the walls survived. We've seen them ourselves.

Talbott Tavern's website describes one of Jesse James's ghostly appearances that was apparently witnessed by two tavern employees—a bookkeeper and a cook. After closing, the two women were taking the day's receipts to the safe—an appropriate time for one of America's most famous robbers to show up. The pair saw a man in a long black frock coat walking across the landing at the top of the stairs. Curious, they followed the strange figure upstairs and saw him exit through the fire escape door. Frightened but determined, the women opened the door—and there he stood. The man turned around, looked at them, and "let out a hideous laugh" before disappearing. Poof! Although the witnesses had the day's receipts in hand, James made no attempt to rob them. Perhaps he didn't want to upset the management, or maybe in death, money just didn't mean much to him anymore. The women didn't recognize the ghost's face at first. Then, three weeks later, the bookkeeper was watching a TV special on the outlaw and recognized Jesse James as the man she had seen at the tavern.[3]

Since that sighting, other employees have witnessed James walking the halls. He's wearing the same coat, they say, and laughs the same disturbing laugh. It's odd that the outlaw would haunt a building he never lived in, wasn't murdered in, and never robbed. But he did spend a lot of time at the tavern, so maybe he felt safe there and decided to come back to stay—permanently.

Historic buildings like the Talbott Tavern are favorite haunts for lingering spirits. The tavern, built in 1779, is the oldest western stagecoach stop still open for business. During its heyday, the tavern attracted influential figures and celebrities, including frontiersman Daniel Boone, explorer George Rogers Clark, and future Presidents Jackson, Harrison, and Lincoln.

The inn is named for George Talbott, who bought the tavern in 1886. Tragedy soon struck the family, and within two years, six of Talbott's children had died there. Paranormal author Todd Atteberry says one child tumbled down the stairs, while a lovesick daughter hanged herself. The ghost of a small girl has been spotted scampering around the dining area. Could she be one of the unfortunate Talbott children?[4]

Witnesses say they've seen George Talbott's troubled spirit wandering around, and Mrs. Talbott makes appearances as well. She's a thin woman with long, wavy brown hair who is wearing a white floor-length dress. Mrs. Talbott has been seen floating through the Audubon Dining Room, but when anyone tries to follow her, she vanishes without a trace.

Travel and Leisure magazine says the tavern has a "slightly spooky charm."[5] But Mrs. Talbott has scared off a few overnight visitors. The tavern's website reports that one couple left hurriedly in the middle of the night after waking up to find a woman in white hovering over them. The apparition then turned and floated out the window. Who wouldn't pack up and leave after such an encounter?

One guest reported seeing red, yellow, and white balls of light bouncing around his room one night just months before the 1998 fire. Orbs perhaps? He tried to get out of bed, but he was held down by some invisible force that sent what seemed like electricity coursing through his body, although it didn't hurt.

Todd Atteberry admits to drinking a fair amount of bourbon during one of his stays and going to bed a little feverish. His room was freezing, although he could hear the heat kicking on with clangs and clicks throughout the night. Despite the warm air circulating in the room, Atteberry was shivering under three blankets. However, when he moved to the other bed in his room, Atteberry found it "warm and cozy," and he slept soundly.[6] Atteberry noted other odd occurrences that night, such as footsteps on the stairs at all hours, someone or something knocking on doors, doors slamming shut by themselves, and disembodied voices talking outside his room.

Witnesses have reported weird things happening during the day as well—forks and glasses moving around on the dining room tables, furniture lifting itself off the floor, and shadows emerging from the dark into the light before suddenly disappearing. Then there are the sounds. The tavern's website reports that witnesses have heard music—especially an old piano playing tunes unaccompanied by human hands—and unwound clocks chiming late at night.

Sadly, there were no mischievous spirits around when Marie and her sisters stayed at the tavern in the 1990s. And our more recent tour was uneventful in the ghostly sense. However, over the years, other ghost-seeking tourists have recorded orbs and other ghostly apparitions and posted them on pattistarr.com. Images taken in Pioneer Cemetery include photos of shadow people, the misty form of a Blue Man spirit, and the faint outline of a woman rising up from the ground. One photo captured the ghostly face of a little girl between two walkers, even though there were no children on the tour that day. A few spirits have posed in the tavern with the ghost hunters. Other sightings include a face in the TV and the misty shape of a little girl swinging in a chandelier. Next door at the Jailer's Inn, one of the ten most haunted places in America, according to the Travel Channel, Patti Starr and her pals have captured a picture of a ghost boy, ghosts shrouded in a dark mist, and spirit orbs around the stockade out front.

Sometimes haunted locations are close to home—like Eastern Kentucky University in Richmond, where we live. Mason and our oldest son, Mitchell, followed Patti Starr on a campus ghost tour one Halloween in pursuit of the Blue Lady, who is said to haunt the 145-seat Pearl Buchanan Theatre in the Keen Johnson Building. The story of the Blue Lady, which doesn't appear in any university records, involves a female student cast in the title role of Henrik Ibsen's *Hedda Gabler.* Apparently, playing the part of the vicious and ultimately suicidal Hedda made the student so depressed that she committed suicide herself before opening night. Supposedly, she can occasionally be seen floating across the stage in a blue dress, eternally awaiting her opening night. Mitchell and several other attendees managed to photograph a few blue orbs on the lower left side of the stage. Even if they were only dust motes, it's interesting that a variety of people using different types of cameras captured the same-colored orbs in the same location.

Nationally, ghost-walk customers like us can experience spooky spots by candlelight, flashlight, or streetlight as our guides shuttle us around graveyards, abandoned asylums, lighthouses, historic homes, and anywhere tragedies have occurred. The tours are usually led by amateur historians and actors, and they usually take place at night, when our imaginations are more likely to run wild. So, along with the dark tales of murder and mayhem, these tours offer a smattering of history about the people and places involved.

Researchers from Goldsmith College, University of London, claim that in addition to being lucrative, ghost tours can be therapeutic because "they help us talk about and process violent pasts" and deal with death and tragedy. We are "encouraged to essentially laugh in the face of death." Although the violence associated with most hauntings happened to real people, the researchers observe that "using the creepy lens of ghosts as a subject adds a paranormal distance or façade to death." Blending history with hauntings helps us explore our past and speculate about our future. "Through tales of death a city's history is brought to life but in a way that is more entertaining than mournful because of the uncanny nature of ghosts," the researchers concluded. Guides "turn tragic history into high-spirited entertainment."[7]

There are plenty of restless spirits wandering around Kentucky. If you see a tall, gloomy apparition in an outdated tuxedo and cape strolling through Louisville's Central Park at dusk, it's probably Alfred Victor DuPont, or Uncle Fred. He's related to the Delaware DuPonts, who made a fortune in gunpowder, chemicals, and rubber. There were too many relatives involved with the family business in Delaware, so Fred and his brother Biderman moved to Louisville in the 1850s to start new ventures in Kentucky. Hauntedhouses.com says Biderman bought the land that's now Central Park and lived there with his wife and seven kids. He developed the property into a recreation area with a playground, lake, roller coaster, and art museum, cordially inviting the public to attend picnics, concerts, and fireworks on the grounds.

In 1879 the brothers built a three-story, ten-bedroom mansion on Fourth Street for bachelor Fred to live in and where other family members could stay when they visited Louisville for business or pleasure. It now operates as a bed-and-breakfast. We've stayed there ourselves, mainly because it was advertised as "haunted."

Despite having access to this palatial home, Fred preferred to stay at the downtown Galt House Hotel. It gave Fred more privacy to pursue his dalliances, especially with Maggie Payne, who ran an upscale bordello that Fred frequented. When Maggie shared the news of her pregnancy with Fred on May 16, 1893, he didn't do the honorable thing and acknowledge his paternity, propose marriage, or even offer financial help. That was a deadly mistake. Maggie, outraged by Fred's unchivalrous response, shot him in the heart several times in broad daylight on the porch of the Galt House, with witnesses around.

At first, it seemed that Maggie's baby would soon become an orphan, since she would surely be convicted of murdering Fred in cold blood. But the DuPonts cared more about saving face than seeking justice. So they paid the coroner, the police, and the local newspaper to cover up the scandal and list the official cause of Fred's death as a heart attack. That ruse left Maggie in the clear, and she never faced trial. The truth wasn't made public until the 1930s.

As time passed, it seems that Uncle Fred had a change of heart in the afterlife. His wanderings through Central Park are said to be a search for the child he never knew. Like a good host, Fred also makes the occasional appearance at his former home on Fourth Street. A workman renovating the house in 1998 reportedly saw a man fitting Fred's description wearing an old-fashioned tux with a bloodstain and a bullet hole near the heart. The apparition then just faded away.

However, it seems that Fred is up to his old tricks with the ladies. He allegedly got "handsy" with a female interior decorator at the B&B—grabbing her buttocks and breathing in her ear. Luckily for Fred, she didn't have her trusty revolver locked and loaded. Mostly, though, Fred doesn't bother the B&B guests. On January 15, 2012, Marie published a *Richmond Register* column about our overnight experience there. We didn't hear any creaking stairs or mournful moaning, and we certainly heard no pleading for mercy. We were awakened by airplanes flying overhead, but we can't blame Fred for his home being so close to the Louisville airport. Even if nothing happens on our ghost tours or overnight stays, we still love the possibility that something supernatural *could* occur.

On his website, Todd Atteberry describes his own love for haunted places this way:

> There's only one way you'll ever believe in the paranormal. [And that way is] if you see something with your own eyes, or hear a story that makes you believe. If EVPs [electronic voice phenomena] were going to prove the existence of a great beyond, Zak Bagans [host of the Travel Channel's *Ghost Adventures*] would have the Nobel Prize by now. I go to haunted places, and I love a haunted inn, pub or hotel where I can sit and soak up the atmosphere. There are places where you can feel that something might happen at any moment. And that my friends, is the best you can hope for.[8]

It's a classic human desire to seek new adventures, to face the unknown, to shine a light into the darkness, to walk down an abandoned pathway to see what's at the end of it. Despite our fears, we're willing to fly to the moon, dive deep into the ocean, and dig through the remains of ancient civilizations to satisfy our curiosity. It's why people become explorers, scientists, researchers, historians, writers, and poets. And it's why many of us take ghost tours. We'll probably keep snapping pictures in haunted spots, even though we know that the orbs are likely just digital artifacts. But if we ever discover just one genuine ghost orb, that could be a game changer.

DARK TOURISM

Hauntings at the Anderson Hotel and Buffalo Trace Distillery

Since you're reading this book, chances are you're a "dark tourist." According to a 2019 *Washington Post* article, dark tourists are drawn to sites of tragedies, atrocities, accidents, natural disasters, death, suffering, violence, and murder.[1] Tourism writers cite about nine hundred places in 112 countries that fall into this category, including Alcatraz in San Francisco, Checkpoint Charlie in Berlin, and Chernobyl in Ukraine.

An attraction to the ghoulish is hardly new. People have gathered to witness public hangings across America, view gladiator contests in Rome's Colosseum, and tour Jack the Ripper's neighborhood in Whitechapel, England. But these days, Kentucky cities like Louisville, Lexington, and Bardstown are cashing in on this phenomenon because dark tourists often visit other attractions while they're in the area; they eat at restaurants, fill up their tanks with gas, and stay overnight at hotels or Airbnbs. And they buy T-shirts, coffee mugs, and souvenir key rings.

In 2023 Kentucky's Department of Tourism launched "Kentucky After Dark." The state spent $200,000 to promote twelve paranormal destinations around Halloween. The following year, the number of spooky sites increased to twenty. The haunted Anderson Hotel in Lawrenceburg was one of the stops both years, so we decided to attend a ghost-hunting seminar led by paranormal investigator and author Jeff Waldridge, who manages the place.

No one bothered to tidy up before we got there. In fact, the peeling paint, threadbare chairs and couches, stained mattresses, shabby rug, and well-worn linoleum floors screamed neglect. It was like whoever was in charge just turned off the lights, walked out the door, and never came back.

That's partially true. The hotel, built in the mid-1930s, never had much of a heyday, and it closed in the 1980s. Lawrenceburg is in the Bourbon Distillery District, but according to Waldridge, tourism didn't pick up after Prohibition, leaving the hotel in the lurch. It fell on hard times in the 1950s, when it became a flophouse where people could rent a room for $2 a day (equivalent to $30 in today's economy). Waldridge says that in addition to a few regular residents, many of them elderly, the hotel attracted folks who were down on their luck, such as gamblers, prostitutes, and those fresh out of prison or a mental institution. It wasn't the safest place to stay, and several boarders kept golf clubs, sticks, and wooden boards behind their doors to use as weapons against intruders. Even at $2 a day, many residents couldn't pay their bills, so the landlord would change the locks and keep whatever was inside. That accounts for the forty-plus years of tattered furniture remaining in the rooms and even some family photos still in the frames.

At least thirteen people have died on the premises, including three suicides and some who died of natural causes. Waldridge says he's seen about ten apparitions—some solid, some see-through, and some smoky—in the approximately five hundred hours he's spent investigating the hotel. A phantom lady walking down the stairs seemed remarkably realistic even to his trained eye. He also spotted a legless man in the hallway who walked on his hands (with handprints on the carpet to prove it). Waldridge investigated a woman who committed suicide in one room and found "Bible verses taped on the wall, in adult handwriting, written with crayon." Then there was the "Burning Man," who appeared to be ablaze from the waist up; this may be a spirit from the 1800s, when there was a fire in the funeral home that occupied the site. The "Hanging Man" has been seen in the room where a high school senior hanged himself in a closet. Whenever Waldridge takes groups into that room, it's obvious the spirit doesn't like women and refuses to answer their questions. Several mean-spirited entities have lingered and express their dislike for visitors of any kind. "I've seen people scratched. I've seen them receive bite marks—human bite marks—while in the hotel," Waldridge writes in *The Haunting of a Bourbon Town*, coauthored with John Cosper.[2]

Unlike TV investigators, who travel with a full crew and all kinds of ghost-hunting gadgets (and, according to Waldridge, stage many of their cases), Waldridge travels light—and alone. During our seminar he demonstrated a few of the contraptions used in the ghost-hunting business, but Waldridge packs only a voice recorder, an EMF (electromagnetic field) meter, and sometimes a plasma ball to detect and attract spirits. Plasma balls, otherwise known as Tesla globes, generate static electricity to create a beautiful lightning-like display inside a glass sphere. Waldridge suggested that spirits might be able to draw energy from such a device, but a Reddit thread concerning this claim got a rather curt reply from Thumper1k92: "We don't know. There isn't enough evidence about paranormal entities, revenants, spirits, ghosts, etc. to say if they even need energy or can acquire energy. Anyone who tells you otherwise is trying to sell you something."[3] We admit we were gullible enough to buy a plasma ball. No spirits have materialized yet, but the static-electric discharge fascinates our cats.

Waldridge prefers to use a voice-activated recorder so he doesn't have to listen to hours of overnight recordings in the hopes of finding something useful. On our ghost hunt, for example, we allowed a number of seconds to elapse between questions, but because the ghosts were quiet that day, the playback went instantly from question to question. As a purist, Waldridge doesn't remove the hisses and pops in his recordings, claiming that it taints the process. "I slow it down or bring up the volume, but otherwise don't tamper with it." Another thing Waldridge refuses to do is become an "orb chaser." Orbs are probably just dust motes that create artifacts in our cameras, rather than floating balls of energy from lost spirits. Clients who believe in orbs "don't need an exorcism," Waldridge jokes. "They need a Hoover." Likewise, Waldridge believes shadow people are often just optical illusions.

A law enforcement officer by profession, the semiretired Waldridge calls himself an "accidental historian" who combs through old newspapers to discover the history of a place, or he gathers anecdotal accounts if that doesn't satisfy his curiosity. "Knowing the history can help you connect the dots and identify who those visions and voices belong to," he says.

Waldridge uses a slightly different set of ghostly categories than Grant Wilson. According to Waldridge, there are basically three types of hauntings: residual, intelligent, and demonic. A residual haunting is like watching a replay of a recording. The spirit says something that has been said before in the same way, but the spirit is unable to say anything new or react to questions. His personal example is a full-bodied apparition of a twenty-something man with greasy hair wearing grunge-style clothes—flannel shirt and jeans. He just stares at the floor or wall, unaware of his surroundings. The spirit is gone in a flash once somebody spots him.

In an intelligent haunting, the spirit can move things and interact with the living. Waldridge told us that when addressing ghosts, we should keep our questions simple and open-ended. And never ask spirits how they died. "They might not know they're dead," he says. (And the shock might kill them?) Also, when communicating with ghosts, don't ask them to speak into the recorder, since they may be unfamiliar with that term. Instead, say, "Can you speak into the little black box in my hand?"

Waldridge claims to be sensitive to the presence of spirits and experiences a wave of vertigo when they're around. He's always looking for ways to connect with them and convince them to communicate with him. While recording an electronic voice phenomenon (EVP) in the "Drunk Room," which contained empty bottles of Ancient Age bourbon, Waldridge asked the spirit what he did all day long. He answered, "I drink." So Waldridge brought him some bourbon, rum, and vodka. Waldridge then asked what the spirit wanted to drink that night. When he played back the audio recording, he heard the ghost answer, "Whiskey."

Waldridge's third type of haunting is demonic. He emphatically warns amateurs and professionals alike not to open the door to demons. You'll be sorry if you do. During his investigation of such cases, Waldridge has heard growls and seen toys tossed around a room, and some type of entity reportedly cut his finger. So Waldridge takes every precaution possible before responding to a demonic case. He has his car blessed beforehand, packs holy water, and brings along a protective St. Benedict coin. "Don't battle the devil yourself. Call a trained exorcist," he insists.

Waldridge isn't the only one who cautions ghost hunters to be careful. He cites the book cowritten by John Zaffis, *Shadows in the Dark*, which describes the dangers of encountering evil energy during paranormal investigations. Zaffis, who specializes in demonology, argues that demonic victims are dealing with real phenomena, not mass hallucinations or hoaxes. Not everyone is convinced, however. Zaffis describes his frustration with nonbelievers. "All it takes is one person not even involved in the case who has no idea what is occurring in the home to say it is a hoax, and then it is considered to actually be a hoax," Zaffis says. "I could never understand this. This debunker just says the word *hoax* and it's taken as truth."[4]

Interestingly, Zaffis is the nephew of Ed Warren—half of the paranormal investigating team of Ed and Lorraine Warren, whose cases were spun into horror movies such as *The Conjuring*, *Annabelle*, and *The Amityville Horror.* Before the Warrens' deaths (Ed in 2006 and Lorraine in 2019), skeptics denounced the couple as frauds. "While their skills at exorcism are debatable, their skill at self-promotion remains unmatched."[5]

Still, people continue to report evil spirits. When dealing with demons, Waldridge offers this warning: if you find something wrapped in burlap, leave it alone. Paranormal researchers claim that the rough, all-natural texture of burlap can absorb and hold evil. So whatever is tied up in that burlap bag might be something evil that needs to stay contained. Waldridge cautions that an evil spirit that's released can cause bad dreams or can convince someone to do dangerous things.

Also, be wary of antiques and cursed objects, which might have negative forces attached to them. Waldridge has a possessed Annabelle doll that looks like a harmless Raggedy Ann, but he won't touch it unless he's wearing welding gloves. He also has a hand-painted clown bank from the 1970s or 1980s that terrorized its former owners. Its head was broken off and glued back on, and the clown's balloons are missing. Although the clown has never done anything evil, Waldridge says it has been known to move around by itself, set off the EMF meters, and play with people's hair and legs.

Disappointingly, we didn't encounter any residual or intelligent entities during our seminar and ghost tour. And thankfully, we didn't meet any demonic spirits either. No one wants to be bitten, slapped, scratched, or even touched during one of these outings. However, we spent several hours at the Anderson Hotel on a cold spring day, and the abandoned, unheated building was quite chilly, so the tour definitely gave us the shivers!

One positive outcome of his ghost hunting is that Jeff Waldridge met his future wife, who shares his enthusiasm for all things supernatural. She helped him turn the Anderson Hotel into a staged haunted house one October.

What better place for a Kentucky spirit to haunt than a distillery? Though we never acquired a taste for bourbon, we've taken many distillery tours over the years. One of our favorite stops is the 130-acre Buffalo Trace campus overlooking the Kentucky River in Frankfort. It has been around since 1792 and is the oldest continuously operating distillery in the United States.

Our Halloween 2019 ghost tour started at Stony Point Mansion, the home of Colonel Albert Blanton, who died in the house in 1959. Blanton started doing odd jobs at what was then the George T. Stagg Distillery when he was just sixteen years old. By the time he turned twenty-four, he had worked in every department at the distillery. This whiz kid eventually reached the top of the ladder and was named president of the company in 1921.

According to the Buffalo Trace Distillery website, in his fifty-five years of service, Blanton helped the business thrive under adverse conditions. During Prohibition, when many distilleries closed, Blanton kept his company afloat by securing one of the few licenses granted to produce "medicinal whiskey." Doctors and even veterinarians could prescribe medicinal whiskey to treat whatever real or imagined ailment their patients suffered from. Blanton also navigated the distillery through the Great Depression and the disastrous 1937 flood (which shut down operations for just one day), plus the daunting days of World War II.[6] By the time he retired in 1952, Blanton had expanded the operation from 44 buildings to its current 114. He also added some aesthetic touches, such as gorgeous gardens, and a clubhouse for social events.

After pouring his heart and soul into making bourbon, Blanton is apparently still watching over the business. On our tour, the guide explained the whiskey's aging process, which involves storing the bourbon in charred oak barrels in rickhouses, and then shared a story about another guide who saw a man in nineteenth-century attire studying a rack of barrels with great interest. Unsure how the strangely dressed person had gotten separated from the group, the guide asked the man to rejoin the tour. Instead, he walked between—and through—the stout barrels stacked to the ceiling and then vanished. As our guide pointed out, it was obvious that a grown man of any size could not fit through that tiny space. But the ghost of Colonel Blanton, checking on his beloved bourbon, managed to do it.

The former president, who died seven years after his retirement, also stops by his office occasionally. One wintery morning a newly arrived worker was hanging up her coat in the sun room when she saw "a tall, dark figure pass by on her right." She quickly reached for the light switch to see who was there but found herself alone—with no sign of an intruder. She told paranormal investigator Patti Starr, who was checking out odd occurrences at the distillery in 2017: "Colonel Blanton was a tall, thin man, and the fact that he died in this same room made me think that maybe he was still making his rounds in the manor. I was okay with that thought and proceeded to get ready for the day's business."

When Starr is on a spirit hunt, she tries to ignore background information that might influence her investigation of any unusual activity. She and her team hit the jackpot in the basement of Stony Point. The EMF meters were beeping and flashing like crazy, which signals a disturbance. Starr politely asked the entity to answer some questions for her. Using a method called "electric dowsing," Starr instructed the spirit to answer with one beep for yes and silence for no. When the session was over, the results indicated that the spirit was Colonel Blanton.

While Starr was chatting with Blanton's ghost, her former student Bobbie Vereeke was in a back office in a mild trance. Vereeke has a rare talent for automatic writing, which is when a spirit takes control of her hand and scribbles out messages. Apparently, Anna, a former housekeeper, jotted down comments about what a great man Blanton was and how much everyone wanted to please him. Anna sticks around the distillery because, she said, "I don't have anywhere else to go."

These aren't the only spirits floating around Buffalo Trace. A 2017 *Kentucky Monthly* article by Brent Owen tells the story of a foreman who was napping in Warehouse C one day. That's where they keep racks and racks of those heavy barrels of bourbon as they age to maturity. He was awakened by a voice warning him to get his crew out of the warehouse. He looked around and saw no one, so he tried to catch a few more winks. However, the voice jolted him awake again, more forcefully this time, commanding him to "get your men out of there now!" The foreman responded this time, telling his crew to take a break. Once they had left, part of the building collapsed—right where the men had been working. The life-saving warning was believed to come from E. H. Taylor, Blanton's predecessor, although both men were known to be concerned for the safety of their employees. Owen's article also mentions sightings of ghostly children on the premises, including a little girl climbing a tree next to Blanton's mansion. Owen believes she could be one of two neighbor girls who died—one "drowned in a well, and the other died of a fever."[7]

Liz Carey, a travel writer for Roadtrippers.com, mentions other spookiness at the distillery, such as lights in the closed gift shop; footsteps above the gift shop, as if several big guys wearing heavy boots were stomping around up there; something being dragged across the floor; and noises and voices coming from a former meeting room that was empty. Carey relates an incident recalled by tour guide Lindsey Brewer that gave her chills: "I was giving a tour . . . and there were about 30 of us in the rickhouse," she says. "I had just been talking about the ghosts, and I heard a voice over my shoulder say, 'Rye.' I looked around and there was no one there. So I asked the group, 'Did you hear that?' All 30 of them said they'd heard it too."[8]

So the next time you visit a Kentucky distillery, don't be surprised if you hear stories about ghostly men in the warehouse or exiting the elevator or appearing in windows where no one is supposed to be. None of the reports indicate that these spirits are angry, vengeful, or rude. Distillery wraiths seem to be rather mellow. You may even hear about a male spirit dressed in nineteenth-century clothing who is seen sitting at a table enjoying a bottle of ghostly bourbon. He pours, lifts the glass, sips, smiles, and slowly fades away.

THE SEARCH FOR APPALACHIAN GHOSTS

One active thread on Reddit.com asks readers to respond to the question: Are the Appalachian Mountains haunted? "I hear lots of things," writes one woman, "like people won't whistle at night, won't look out their windows at night, and if you hear your name at night, you ignore it even if it sounds like a neighbor."[1] The inquiry generated some stereotypical responses. Some claimed that folks in the hollers tell these stories "to keep people out so we can be left alone." This desire for privacy may be due to a distrust of outsiders, or perhaps it's to prevent anyone from accidentally stumbling onto someone's "business venture." Some responders mentioned moonshine stills and marijuana patches, but of course, such illegal activities are hardly unique to Appalachia. Others suggested that such tales are spread by local tourism officials and business owners looking to make money by promoting supernatural tours.

R. Zackery Youngblood collected a number of ghost stories from his home in southern Appalachia as part of an academic study. His observations seem relevant to our search for similar spirit tales specific to Kentucky's Appalachian region: "In collecting stories from various individuals living in Southern Appalachia (primarily northeast Tennessee), I found that each story was grounded in a place. Usually, these places were described very specifically. None of the stories I obtained were of hauntings or ghosts that were more general or followed individuals around. Instead, each story had a grounded, real-world location with which it was associated."[2]

The distinct aspects of the Appalachian region and its culture suggest that ghost stories there should be rooted in the geography of the mountains. A true Appalachian ghost story should be homegrown rather than an imported folktale motif from England, Wales, Scotland, or Ireland, where the ancestors of many Appalachians came from.

Let's start with a story from McCreary and Whitley Counties, where Raven Willow tells the tale of "The Ghost Bride of Cumberland Falls." We've stayed at Cumberland Falls State Resort Park many times, but unlike some other visitors, we've never seen a young, semitransparent woman in a bridal dress standing near the falls. Willow relates the background of these ghost sightings:

> The "ghost bride" story dates back into the 1950s, when a young bride and groom came to Cumberland Falls State Park for their honeymoon and [were] staying at DuPont Lodge. The young bride was fascinated with the large waterfall and insisted that her photo be taken with the beautiful falls in the background. The couple found an overlook just a few hundred feet from the falls that would provide for the most beautiful photo. As the bride stood on the cliffs at the edge of the 75-to-80-foot escarpment, she lost her balance and fell to her death. The groom was so distraught and heartbroken that he almost immediately jumped from the cliff to join her.[3]

Willow writes that visitors who walk down to the overlook in the evening have spotted the bride, but like many wraiths that value their privacy, she dissolves into thin air if anyone approaches her. Visitors to the park have also reported hearing howls near the falls, presumably the bride screaming as she plunges to her death. And guests and employees have seen the spirit in the rooms and corridors of DuPont Lodge.

One employee who was cleaning up around the falls reported hearing a sickening *thud*, as if someone had struck the rocks at the base of the cliff. The worker checked but saw no broken body on the rocks. Instead, she noticed white flower petals showering down, one by one. This was in late autumn, when few plants were in bloom, but she counted at least twenty petals floating on the breeze and settling on the wet stones and in the swift-moving water.

Cumberland Falls is famous for moonbows that occur several times a year. These unusual lighting effects might account for the curious sightings in the swirling mists of the falls at night. Also, ghostly brides are not uncommon in folklore collections around the world. In fact, there's nothing particularly Appalachian about this story—except that its setting is near Corbin in eastern Kentucky.

Another posting on the Reddit thread notes:

> There are a lot of ghost stories. I believe some of them may be more true than we know, but I don't think there is anything supernatural going on. For whatever reason, a lot of folks in Appalachia just seem scared of the woods. They won't go out without a gun; they think that there are cryptids, or they are just terrified of snakes or coyotes. Combine that with cultural trauma, poor access to good information, poverty, and a long and rich tradition of storytelling, and you get a lot of widespread ghost stories. That being said, there are places in Appalachia where you should be wary of wandering around the woods, even on public property. Not because of ghosts or snakes, but because of sketchy people doing illicit things in the woods.[4]

This Reddit posting mentions Appalachia's "long and rich tradition of storytelling." That idea is echoed by Patrick W. Gainer, author of *Witches, Ghosts, and Signs: Folklore of the Southern Appalachians*:

> On long winter evenings there was a time to gather before the fireplace to sing songs and tell stories, and to exchange ideas. If a stranger came by, he was welcome to stay the night and sit at the board [dinner table] with the family for a good supper and breakfast. Stories were told of ghosts and witches, of pioneer days and unusual incidents. The stories of witches and ghosts were not told so much to make others believe in these things, but because these stories were an entertaining feature of the oral literature of the folk. Our society today needs books, recordings, radio, and television for our entertainment and knowledge, for we retain very little in our minds to pass on to others. There is very little remaining in our modern society in the way of oral tradition. Our pioneer ancestors, however, did not need books as much as our society needs them. For they preserved in their minds a treasury of knowledge, of fiction, of poetry as song, ready to be passed on to their children and grandchildren.[5]

If these stories are really "the oral literature of the folk," as Gainer suggests, the region should have its own version of many classic tall tales and supernatural legends. Collections of folktales, such as Leonard W. Roberts's *South of Hell-fer-Sartin: Kentucky Mountain Folk Tales*, catalog examples of folk literature—stories told for entertainment—such as "Rawhead and Bloodybones," "The Big Black Toe," and "Jack and the Miller's Daughter."[6]

But our investigation isn't about collecting stories told for entertainment. We're interested in what author Bill Ellis defines as a legend: a narrative told as a true story by a given population "using the extremes of experience, their own and others', to explore, test, and redefine their perspectives on the 'real' world."[7]

A person reciting a legend of "high strangeness" might preface it by saying, "This really happened." But as the story unfolds, the "realness" becomes a bit fuzzy. These stories are usually set in the real world, at a specific time and place, not in the once-upon-a-time realm of a fairy tale. But the events described in that "real" world exist in the shadow area between what is physically real and what is psychologically real.

Later in this chapter, we'll share a uniquely Appalachian "true" story—a spooky tale rooted so deeply in the region's culture that it's hard to imagine it being told anywhere else. But to get there, we need to take a brief detour to western Kentucky, where, on February 1, 1910, the Browder underground mine in Muhlenberg County exploded, killing thirty-four men and injuring dozens more. Authorities blamed the disaster on a spark that set off a methane gas explosion. The superheated gas then ignited bags of black powder used for blasting. The death toll was a record for Kentucky, but deaths in underground mines were hardly uncommon in those days. Browder's ventilation fans continued to work after the explosion, and rescue crews were able to enter the mine fairly quickly. All the bodies were recovered and given a proper burial more than a century ago.

Coal mining was and is a dangerous profession. However, some mine operators in early twentieth-century Kentucky cared more about profit than about the safety of their men. When Mason was growing up in Central City, people claimed they could hear trapped miners calling for help from deep below the town. The coal seams under Central City had been mined decades earlier, and rusty grates covered rectangular cement ventilation ducts throughout the city. Standing in the sunbaked weeds overlooking one of these ducts, a person could look down into the darkness and hear water gushing through the long-abandoned shafts. How far down was the water? How many of the mine's galleries were still open? Were there still bodies down there? It wasn't much of a stretch to imagine calls for help coming from the darkened chambers.

Kentucky mines rarely contained large rooms, corridors, or hallways like those in Mammoth Cave. More commonly, miners blasted out a fifty-five-inch-high crack to remove the coal—duck-walking into and out of the low-ceilinged chamber. Hundreds of men labored there in horrifying conditions, and many died suddenly from rockfalls. Many more died slowly from black lung disease caused by continually breathing in coal dust.

Western Kentucky's coalfields once covered Muhlenberg, Ohio, Union, Henderson, Hancock, Webster, and McLean Counties. But by far the largest coalfield in Kentucky encompasses most of the eastern third of the state, stretching across its Appalachian region.

Cassandra Yorgey, writing in *Extempore News*, tells the story of a group of Perry County campers who had an unsettling late-night experience near a mine. First, she sets the scene: "The mountains of Appalachia are filled with abandoned things, and abandoned places. The rich coal mines that once powered the country fell into decline as technology found better and more efficient ways for society [to operate], and the old mines were left behind. Some say the lost souls of the miners who suffered mistreatment are still there, wandering the forgotten sites." According to Yorgey, the campers planned to spend the night near the entrance of an abandoned mine on Four Seams Mountain (named for the four seams of coal it contained). It had been heavily mined in decades past, but now its galleries, which extended for miles into the mountain, lay empty. The campers rolled out their sleeping bags, ate supper, and retired. They were startled awake at about 3:00 a.m. by sounds coming from the mine: "They heard something start clinking. It sounded as if pick-axes were hitting rock, despite the boys being quite sure they were alone," Yorgey writes. "One friend was ready to 'nope' out of the situation and immediately started packing his bag to go, but another friend made a different choice. He chose to go looking for the source of the sound. He went searching with a flashlight, obviously believing it to be a person responsible for the sounds. After the clinking, they believed they heard voices that seemed to be talking but then a loud roar that was almost like screaming, and then silence."[8]

Running for your life seems like a sensible choice when encountering unknown entities in an isolated location with little or no cell service. Venturing into an abandoned mine possibly occupied by ghosts swinging sharp implements is a very bad idea. Sure enough, *all* the campers decided to "nope" out of there in a hurry and lived to tell the tale of the ghostly coal miners still toiling deep inside Four Seams Mountain. If ghost hunters are correct in claiming that spirits get trapped at sites of tragedy and death, then Appalachia's coalfields would certainly be among the most haunted locations in the world.

Yorgey stresses that back in the day, some mines were operated by heartless owners, with little to no state or federal regulation or oversight to ensure the miners' safety. Some mine owners paid workers starvation wages and even forced them to accept payment in company scrip—sometimes paper currency, but often coins called "flickers" that could be spent only at the company store. This practice inspired Rosewood, Kentucky, native Merle Travis's 1947 song "Sixteen Tons," which highlights the desperation of miners who were heavily in debt to the coal companies.

Mining was and remains a major contributor to the area's economy, and in the 1930s, the abuses of the coal companies helped fuel an often deadly struggle to unionize the mine workers. The so-called Harlan County War, which raged throughout this period, claimed an unknown number of lives. Private security guards and law enforcement officers fired on the striking workers, who shot back. The brutality of some of these encounters is heartbreaking. The National Guard and federal troops occupied "Bloody Harlan" on several occasions in an attempt to control the situation.[9] This violent period is remembered today in a number of stories, such as the tale of Headless Annie, told throughout the Black Mountain area.

Steve Gilly and Rod Mullins recount one version of Headless Annie's story on the website Mountain Lore. According to them, an unnamed miner living near Black Mountain was fed up with subsistence pay and deadly working conditions, so he tried to convince his fellow miners to sign union cards. His daring but dangerous effort to organize the workers was immediately reported to the mine operators. The owners allegedly dispatched a team of hired hitmen to kill the ringleader and his family, thereby sending a message to the other men.

Now, we acknowledge that the prospect of mine operators ordering the murder of an entire family raises the question of how "real" this story is. The exchange of gunfire across a picket line is one thing. Killing a family in cold blood is something else entirely. Nevertheless, in the region's folk memory, the explosive violence of the Harlan County War is still so vivid that a tale of outright homicide seems credible.

According to the story, the company's hired thugs abducted the courageous miner, his wife, and their twelve-year-old daughter, Annie. The kidnappers allegedly drove the family to an unknown location on Black Mountain at night and brutally murdered them. The grisly details of this horrific crime vary, and it is unclear how this information came to light. Annie was reportedly forced to watch her parents being murdered before she was raped and killed. All the bodies were then tossed into a deep ravine high on Black Mountain. The corpses were never found, so the family remains on the mountain to this day—neither avenged nor properly buried. "Legend has it that the specter of Annie roams the mountain at night. She has been seen by drivers, supposedly running out in front of cars on the mountain road, scaring drivers in her ghostly form, wearing a white nightdress and with no visible head."[10]

Black Mountain is isolated, but it's not far from Lynch, Kentucky, and the roads up and down the mountain are potholed and rough. Annie's ghost is apparently seeking help for her parents from the passing motorists. But of course, Annie can't tell them what she wants, and she and her parents are far beyond any earthly help.

Ironically, given that Black Mountain is Kentucky's highest point, there's not much to see up there.[11] The summit belongs to the state of Kentucky, but much of the approach is undeveloped private property. If someone driving up there at night encountered a headless girl in a nightdress, what could she actually be? A ghost? A psychological meme dredged from cultural memory? Or a transdimensional echo of Kentucky's dark history?

Native Americans supposedly referred to Kentucky as "the dark and bloody ground," and during the 1930s, the eastern coalfields were exactly that. It wasn't until the construction of parkways and interstates in the 1960s that the mind-boggling isolation of eastern Kentucky was eased. Even so, those long decades of reclusiveness left their mark.

Appalachians listening to the story of Headless Annie understand that the *real* monster isn't the ghost of a twelve-year-old girl. Miner families, many of whom fought lifelong battles against the crushing debts owed to the company store, know that the real monster stalking their mountains isn't paranormal at all.

THE TRAGIC TALE OF THE BATTLETOWN WITCH

Tennessee folklorists have told the story of the Bell witch for years. A shape-shifting dog-like creature terrorized the family of John Bell in the tiny frontier town of Adams from 1817 to 1821. The creature hit, pinched, and attacked family members, until Bell became sick and died. Kentucky has its own tragic tale of witchcraft and death, but in this case, the alleged witch was the victim.

Twenty-two-year-old Leah Smock lived in Battletown in Meade County. Her intellect and knowledge of healing frightened her superstitious neighbors so badly that in August 1840, when they caught her alone and vulnerable, they tied her up, tossed her in the family's smokehouse, locked the door, set the building on fire, and watched it burn as she suffered an agonizing death. If this story is true, Leah Smock would be the only person burned alive for witchcraft in North America.[1] (Colonial officials in Salem, Massachusetts, followed British law, which prescribed hanging as the punishment for witchcraft. In 1692, twenty of the accused Salem witches were hanged, and one was pressed to death using heavy rocks.[2])

Few records and no photos survive of Leah, who was described as a beautiful woman with long black hair. But it was obvious that personality-wise, she didn't fit in with her neighbors and was misunderstood and feared. According to Gerald W. Fischer's 2016 book, Leah was well versed in herbology and local healing lore.[3] She learned much of this from her mother, who was also a healer but kept a low profile, as well as from her Cherokee friend Indian Joe and on her own initiative.

Charlie Hicks, writing in the *Meade County Messenger* in 1977, cited elderly resident Shirley "Cowboy" Bennett, who recalled several stories about Leah Smock. "People wouldn't talk about the witch, Leah," Bennett said. "My grandmother would tell me to hush up when I'd ask her about it." He continued, "People always thought she had the witch ways about her, but they weren't for sure until she was 12. She was always ahead of her grade. She just knew things she hadn't been taught. She could even tell about the weather changes. They wouldn't let her go to school anymore. They started watching her."[4] But Annie Hamilton, executive director of the Meade County Tourism Bureau, told us in a phone interview that by age twelve Leah knew more than the teacher, so she quit school willingly. "And she wanted to be out in the woods anyway."

Leah was also considered a seer, as she had predicted the deaths of several local individuals. Fischer argues that Smock's uncanny ability may have contributed to her death. But her powers did not allow her to foresee or avoid her own fate.

Cowboy Bennett recalled that Leah didn't have the best people skills, which got her in trouble, even when she was only trying to help. She once asked to hold an infant who was deathly ill, possibly to use her healing knowledge to cure the child. Leery of Leah's intentions and fearful that she might harm the baby, the parents refused to hand the child over. Leah did not take the rejection well. "You'll be sorry!" she yelled. The baby died shortly thereafter, according to Bennett. Did Leah intend that comment as a curse, or was she just frustrated at being denied the opportunity to help the ill child? We will never know. On another occasion cited by Bennett, a man refused to let Leah touch his two new plow horses. Once again she warned, "You'll be sorry!" The next day, both horses died, possibly from drinking poisoned water, which Leah might have been able to counteract with herbs. Being an agent—real or imagined—in the death of babies and horses didn't sit well with her neighbors. Leah's talent for second sight scared the entire community, and she was also accused of hexing gardens, fields, and other farm animals.

Although reports suggest that Leah possessed considerable power as a healer, she may have suffered from a condition that even she couldn't treat. Today, she might be diagnosed with a personality disorder. She would apparently lash out at people with little provocation, saying hurtful things she might later regret. Leah spent a lot of time alone in the woods, either by choice or because of her difficulty dealing with people.[5] Annie Hamilton, however, doesn't believe Leah suffered from a personality disorder. "She just wouldn't suffer fools gladly."

Still, tensions rose, and malice toward Leah festered. To make matters worse, the Smock family, who made their living as coopers (barrel makers), was involved in a contentious land dispute with neighbors. Leah's father had bought three thousand acres from a land agent a couple of years earlier, but the agent had apparently sold that same property to someone else. So, in addition to the fear caused by Leah's "having the shine," there were hard feelings among the families. But was this animosity and fear enough to drive the neighbors to commit such a heinous crime as burning a young woman to death? Annie Hamilton says the community's large German and French population might have contributed to these indefensible actions. "In France and Germany," she notes, "witches were executed by burning." If the neighbors believed Leah Smock was a witch, then folk wisdom and tradition deemed that she must be burned.

In August 1840 community members saw their chance to rid themselves of Leah. As Cowboy Bennett mentioned, the neighbors had been watching the family's activities. So when they saw the whole family leave home on some excursion except for Leah, who stayed behind to do chores, they took action. The cowards came when Leah was alone and couldn't defend herself. Surprised, outnumbered, and unable to resist, Leah was bound and locked in the smokehouse, which was set on fire. The building burned to the ground with Leah trapped inside. Her chilling screams traveled far, but no one came to her rescue.

When Leah's parents returned to find their daughter dead and their smokehouse reduced to ashes, they were devastated. But they had no clue who was responsible, even though some of the perpetrators boasted about their role in Leah's murder. Still, the killers were never publicly identified, and no charges were ever filed. The Smock family left town a few years later.

For whatever reason, the Smocks buried their daughter in a pasture rather than a church graveyard, although Annie Hamilton told us that Leah was a devout Christian who said her prayers every day. The field, near Battletown, later became known as the Elizabeth Daily Cemetery. Leah's headstone is still visible on a wooded hillside. The stone was carved by a boy she had befriended, whom some described as her fiancé. It reads, "Leah Smock departed this life on Aug. 21 1840, aged 22 years 7 months."[6] There is no mention of her ghastly death or her alleged witch-like powers. At one point, some superstitious people partially unearthed Leah's grave site and refilled it with limestone boulders and heavy gravel in an effort to ensure that she stayed buried. According to

Gerald Fischer and Kay Hamilton, these additional features remain visible to this day. However, this extra precaution was apparently a wasted effort, since Leah's apparition regularly appears above her grave and in the surrounding woods. Witnesses say she has long dark hair and wears a long white dress tied with a black cord at the wrists, waist, and neck. Her ghostly figure seems to float, her feet not touching the ground.[7] Leah's face is often turned away or down, and no one has reported seeing her features.

Kay Hamilton indicates that Leah has also popped up in the hallways of the now closed Battletown Elementary School, located near the Smock family's homestead. Leah's unsettling appearances place her in the ghostly category of an unpleasant specter rather than a noisy poltergeist. Leah never speaks. Nor does she harm any of the witnesses. But everyone who spots her decides at that exact moment that it's time to leave.

Most sightings of Leah at her grave are reported by hunters or hikers who occasionally pass by. Curiosity seekers are not welcome. The grave is not easy to find—or get to—and you risk encountering the poisonous snakes that guard it. In addition, the grave is located on private property peppered with prominently displayed signs that warn, "Keep Out," "No Trespassing," and "Danger." Those who blatantly ignore these signs should be advised that trespassers will be prosecuted. Even if you don't believe in witches, you must respect the power of lawyers. They don't cast spells, but they file hefty lawsuits.

One last caution for anyone who is still determined to visit Leah's grave: don't swipe any souvenirs. If you steal stones from the grave, Leah will follow you home to reclaim her property. Using Leah's favorite catchphrase, you'll be sorry if you remove so much as a pebble from the premises.[8]

Given the fleeting and flimsy facts about Leah Smock, we're left with questions. Was she actually practicing witchcraft, or was she just an exceptionally intelligent young woman well versed in the healing effects of natural herbs whose unconventional ways and quick temper alarmed her community? Fischer argues that it's hard to come up with a definitive answer, given the uncertainty surrounding the practice of witchcraft in early America. Was it meant to be harmful or helpful? For example, herbalists might recite a spell or a prayer when applying a poultice, blurring the line between benevolent healing and demonic spell-casting. The practice in America was particularly complex because it grew from various roots. Fischer writes: "Remnants of the European Old Religion that immigrated to America were influenced by two cultures, Native American and West African, that latter brought to the continent directly by the slave trade and indirectly by the Haitian slave revolt.

At the time of white contact, there were many American Indian beliefs, myths, legends, and occult practices, all active parts of Native American culture. Indian Joe, the Native American friend of Leah Smock, would have been familiar with many of them."[9]

We're left with a lot of uncertainties, but not because of a lack of research. Fischer's book includes eight pages of reference notes. Hamilton's book cites traditions handed down from family members whose ancestors lived in the Battletown area for generations and knew the Smock family personally. Both authors cite not only Meade County historical sources but also interviews with Shirley Brown, Leah Smock's great-great-niece.

In his discussion of the Leah Smock tragedy, Fischer notes that under certain circumstances, a community's *thinking* that a person is a witch could give that person considerable power, which might be either a blessing or a curse. In 1840 the Meade County community deeply feared Leah Smock. Was this fear created by her fierce temper, her strange personality, or her access to knowledge that others didn't have? Fischer says:

> The stories of [reputed American witches such as Marie Leveau or the Bell witch] do not prove the existence of witchcraft, but they do prove these people were believed to be able to control forces beyond the capability of ordinary men and women. The perception of this validated the existence of supernatural forces, and that was enough for many to believe. Once their reputation as witches was substantiated, they became endangered by the very perception they had so carefully cultivated. Whether guilty or innocent, they reaped a bitter harvest produced by the seeds they had sown.[10]

If the community believed that Leah Smock possessed supernatural powers, that belief may have become self-fulfilling.

This is similar to the placebo effect. For instance, in medical trials to gauge the effectiveness of a new drug, half the participants receive the potential miracle drug, while the other half are given a placebo. Studies have found that those receiving the placebo, which should have no impact on their condition, often feel better because they *believe* the medication will produce a positive result. The individual's belief—acting through the poorly understood brain-body connection—creates the improvement in their condition, rather than the medication itself. According to an article in *Harvard Health*:

> "The placebo effect is more than positive thinking—believing a treatment or procedure will work. It's about creating a stronger connection between the brain and body and how they work together," said Professor Ted Kaptchuk of Harvard-affiliated Beth Israel Deaconess Medical Center, whose research focuses on the placebo effect. "Placebos may make you feel better but they will not cure you," he said. "They have been shown to be more effective for conditions like pain management, stress-related insomnia, and cancer treatment side effects like fatigue and nausea."[11]

Many physicians can cite examples of belief becoming reality.

Mason's mother told the story of a God-fearing Muhlenberg County woman back in the late 1950s or early 1960s who became convinced that she had been hexed by another woman—a reputed witch. The victim was unable to eat or sleep and took to her bed. Her family, frantic to find a cure, tried every medical intervention available, including trips to hospitals in neighboring states in search of a diagnosis. All the doctors reported that the woman was perfectly healthy and just needed rest. However, her condition continued to deteriorate, so the desperate family sent for a man from New Orleans who practiced Vodun (or Voodoo), an Afro-Caribbean religion often misrepresented as evil in movies and on TV. The Vodun priest arrived and performed his anti-witch spells at the woman's bedside, and she reportedly recovered. Since the priest was already there, the family asked him to place a powerful counterhex on the woman's attacker. And eerily enough, according to Mason's mom, the alleged witch vanished from Central City. To this day, her fate remains unknown. However, the victim climbed out of bed for the first time in weeks and gradually resumed a normal life. Her family paid the priest's fee in full and in cash. That was a wise decision. You don't stiff a Voodoo priest if you know what's good for you.

This case illustrates the power of belief. The woman and her family believed in witchcraft, perhaps because it's explicitly mentioned in the Bible (see Exodus 22:18, Leviticus 19:26 and 20:27, Deuteronomy 18:10–11, and King Saul's invocation of the Witch of Endor in 1 Samuel 28). Believing she had been hexed, the woman fell ill and did not recover until she believed the original spell had been reversed. At the psychological level, what one believes can be almost indistinguishable from physical reality. Such theories may sound ridiculous, but before we get all high and mighty, wrapped up in the sureness of our twenty-first-century science, we should remember that there's no way of knowing what Leah Smock actually did or was capable of doing. A little historical humility is in order here.

Perhaps because of the passage of time, the current community has decided to embrace Leah Smock. The Battletown Witch Festival, held every October since 2022, honors the tradition of folk wisdom, mountain magic, and wiccan teaching, according to Annie Hamilton. In 2023 the event attracted more than six thousand participants, but there won't be any guided tours of Leah's grave. That's off-limits.

Strange things continue to occur there. Kay Hamilton's book mentions the winter day that some horseback riders came upon the Elizabeth Daily Cemetery. Snow blanketed the graves and headstones and hung in the trees above their heads. However, one grave seemed to be free of snow. Even stranger, when they got closer, they saw the green leaves of a ground-hugging vine of indeterminate species growing over that grave. Elsewhere, the blinding white snow covered everything as far as the eye could see—except for that one grave: Leah Smock's.

Perhaps this is a good time to share a pertinent Argentinean saying: "We don't believe in witches, until, that is, we run into one."[12]

OTHER MONSTERS

BIGFOOT BOOGIE

Is There Really a Squatch in These Kentucky Woods?

No Kentuckian has captured video evidence of Bigfoot lurking around the commonwealth, and it would be hard to miss the giant, hairy, smelly, bipedal creature also known as Sasquatch. So far, no one has produced any Bigfootage as famous as the 59.9-second Patterson-Gimlin film shot in 1967 near Bluff Creek, California. Most of Kentucky's witnesses have caught only brief glimpses of the wild man lumbering near highways, waterways, or forests. Such reports may be terrifying, but they're anything but rare. Kentucky is apparently a very "Squatchy" place.

The national Bigfoot Field Research Organization (BFRO), founded by Matt Moneymaker of *Finding Bigfoot* fame, reports 115 credible Kentucky sightings.[1] Charlie Raymond, who established an independent Kentucky Bigfoot database in 1997, puts that number closer to 400. Raymond has conducted more than 435 interviews about sightings in nearly all 120 counties in Kentucky, with the most double-digit reports coming from Anderson, Bullitt, Carter, and Adair Counties. Many of the reports are from deer hunters, fishers, park rangers, and rural homeowners living near rivers, woodlands, abandoned coal mines, and even ancient Native American burial grounds like those around Henderson and Union Counties.[2]

We hunt for Bigfoot the same way we hunt for ghosts and UFOs: in research libraries, in computer databases, and through interviews conducted during the clear light of day. But we did drive down to Renfro Valley one night in October 2011 to see the *Finding Bigfoot* crew in person. The Animal Planet show's stars and production crew were gathering input on recent Bigfoot sightings. We, along with sixty other Kentuckians, attended a town meeting with Matt Moneymaker, James "Bobo" Fay, Cliff Barackman, and Ranae Holland. To our amazement, nearly half the audience, from kids to adults, volunteered that they had personally seen or heard a Sasquatch. Details ranged from watching a Bigfoot leap a five-foot fence and outrun hunting dogs to hearing it whoop, bellow, howl, or roar to scare away humans. In her column for the *Richmond Register*, Marie wrote, "One person swore he heard hammering near his home and when he went to investigate, he found a Squatch using makeshift tools to dig. That was decades ago. They're probably working with power tools by now."[3]

We didn't share a story at the town meeting because we're not "knowers"—people who have seen the creatures for themselves. However, in 1978, when we were living in Owensboro and working as journalists—Mason at the *Messenger-Inquirer* newspaper and Marie at Cable Channel Two TV and WVJS radio stations—there were reports of Bigfoot sightings on Fairview Drive. Something huge, hulking, and hairy had been scaring the residents for a while. It was most noticeable at night, when a horrible odor likened to wet dog, rotten eggs, skunk, or sulfur was evident. (Barton Nunnelly, in his 2017 book *Mysterious Kentucky*, describes the smell of most Squatches as "like rotting corpses" or death.[4]) Marie recalls sitting on someone's roof, keeping watch with a fellow reporter one weekend night, but the evening was disappointingly uneventful, as Bigfoot was a no-show. However, some residents in that Owensboro neighborhood armed themselves and formed a posse to patrol the area. Shots were fired, but apparently the bullets missed their intended target.

This scenario has played out a number of times in different communities. A sighting is reported—perhaps a lone Squatch seen crossing a highway late at night. People get excited, searches are organized, and sometimes shots are fired at a vague outline in the woods. But no compelling evidence is found. Even the national TV crew, equipped with thermal imagers, infrared cameras, and night-vision goggles, couldn't locate any physical traces of the elusive Bigfoot after nine seasons.

We've collected some of the most interesting witness reports to share here. If the reports seem short and rather fragmentary, we agree. To take the next step in Bigfoot research, we need a body—not a fuzzy picture or a tuft of mysterious hair. We need an actual biological specimen.

Kentucky witnesses have offered varied descriptions of the creature they've seen: standing seven to eight feet tall, weighing up to five hundred pounds, having glowing red or green eyes, and covered in white, gray, brown, or reddish brown fur that is long, nappy, greasy, shaggy, shiny, stringy, or frizzy. Picture Chewbacca from *Star Wars*. Bigfoot was the inspiration for that character.

Barton Nunnelly and his family lived in a rural part of Henderson County near the Green River. One day, his brother Dean spied a creature standing behind their farmhouse. "It was muscular and tall," Nunnelly writes, "with a square jaw and small, close-set eyes. It was covered in reddish gray hair, thin and patchy in spots as if it was very old." One morning, some kids saw the creature while waiting for the school bus. "It was standing in a cornfield out front. It towered above the full-grown corn and seemed to sway slightly from side to side as it stood there."[5]

According to Bigfoot researchers, the creatures aren't nocturnal, as some believed, but they usually stay on the move. It's too risky to remain in one place for too long. Charlie Raymond told us that Squatches might sleep only four to six hours at a time in a makeshift bed of natural materials, with a sentry standing guard to watch for intruders. They're also masters of camouflage. Like *Star Trek*'s cloaking devices that can hide an entire starship, Bigfoots have the uncanny ability to "slip behind a tree and in the blink of an eye they can disappear," according to Raymond. This stems from years of adaptation, as Squatches learned to stay motionless for long periods to avoid detection. Raymond told us about one Bigfoot that was covered in leaves. Hikers passing by didn't notice the invisible creature until it got up and ran away.

Most reports are of single males who might be out seeking a mate or foraging for food. Squatches scavenge around gardens and fields and in dumpsters. They might raid a chicken coop or track down deer and elk, which are plentiful. During our interview with Charlie Raymond, he mentioned a woman who spotted a Bigfoot with its arms full of apples from the tree in her yard. Raymond also shared a documented case of a Bigfoot retrieving roadkill. A woman driving along I-75 toward Ohio slowed down when she saw a creature kneeling over a deer carcass, which it scooped up, hefted onto its back, and then ran away.

Sometimes Squatches are bold enough to steal food right off a porch. One family hung some deer meat and a country ham from the ceiling of their porch and later saw a Bigfoot running away with both. In mid-October 1980 a Fleming County woman reported that a white-haired Bigfoot raided her family's back porch freezer in Fairview, apparently opening the lid with its hands and making off with a frozen chicken, two loaves of bread, and a package of hot dogs. The still-frozen chicken was found later, partially eaten.[6]

Squatches also accept handouts. One woman regularly put out pancakes for them—syrup and all. Oddly enough, Bigfoots have reciprocated by leaving gifts for humans, such as persimmons, feathers, kittens, small turtles, arrowheads, or piles of stones.

Though rare, there have been occasional sightings of female Bigfoots, as well as young ones. Raymond's Kentucky Bigfoot website mentions a Boy Scout campout in 1991 during a reenactment of the Civil War Battle of Perryville. A scout heard a rustle in the tree line and saw what he thought was an Ewok—a furry, three-foot-tall creature from *Star Wars*. When he called to a friend, the creature ran away. In hindsight, the scout believes what he saw was actually a young Squatch.

Nunnelly reports that Bigfoots apparently prefer to engage with women rather than men. He recounts the time a tall, hairy, scary monster with glowing green eyes approached his wife, young daughter, and sister as they were gathering laundry from the clothesline at their home in Reed. They ran into the house, locked the door, and hid, relieved that the Squatch didn't try to enter.[7]

For the most part, encounters with Sasquatches are brief and peaceful. According to Raymond, eyewitnesses report that both Squatch and human are more curious and surprised than afraid. After a brief staring contest, the Squatch usually saunters off in one direction, while the human quickly moves off the other way. For example, in Anderson County near Taylorsville Lake, locals sighted a friendly Bigfoot they called "Howdy," who appeared in the 1960s and again in 2011. Raymond says Howdy earned his name by raising his hand like he was waving at people before disappearing back into the woods.

Oddly enough, for a populated and heavily agricultural area, Anderson County is a hot spot for Squatch hunters. In fact, Lawrenceburg hosts a Wildman Days Festival each June to celebrate the area's Bigfoot activity. The festival's website says, "Sightings of the beast known as Bigfoot date back to the late 1700s in Anderson County. We are happy!"[8]

However, not everyone is happy about a Bigfoot infestation. Nunnelly writes that for much of 1975, when he was nine years old and his family had just moved to Spottsville, they were harassed by one or more Bigfoots.[9] "My parents didn't realize that for the next 11 months we would be terrorized by a giant, hairy, red-eyed creature that would later come to be known as 'The Spottsville Monster.'"[10] They were subjected to high-pitched, blood-curdling screams, moans, grunts, whistles, hoots, and mournful noises that sounded like something from "the pits of Hell." Nunnelly's sister also spotted a Squatch as it walked by their kitchen window in Reed in 1971. It escaped into the back fields when Nunnelly's father chased it with his gun.[11]

Still, Raymond says combative encounters are rare. He stresses that Bigfoots are "unaggressive to a fault" and notes that there has been "no documented case in the past 100 years of Squatches doing deliberate harm to a person."[12] Yet Raymond acknowledges that Bigfoots are territorial, and any acts of aggression might just be their way of telling humans to leave the area because they have dibs on it. Matt Moneymaker's BFRO site acknowledges that territorial conflicts can cause Bigfoots to stalk or harass humans in forested areas. Even so, "such confrontations may trigger intimidating displays, growling, etc., but not a physical attack."[13]

Sadly, an encounter at Mammoth Cave National Park in July 2019 clearly shows that humans are more aggressive than Bigfoots. Ben Tobin, writing in the *Louisville Courier-Journal*, reports that Brad Ginn, age twenty-four, and Madelyn Durand, age twenty-two, noticed a man and a young boy passing their campsite late one night. The man said he was hunting Bigfoot—with a pistol. "A few minutes later we see their lights approaching again," Ginn said, "and as they get closer we hear the man yell something like, 'Oh my God! Do you see that? There it is!'" From their tent, Durand and Ginn watched as the man "shot his gun into the darkness." According to Ginn, the man said "he saw Sasquatch emerge from the brush near our tent and start approaching him."[14] Apparently, no one was injured, but this incident shows why Bigfoot hunting can be hazardous—the danger coming mainly from humans. When a Bigfoot gets scared, it disappears into the woods. When humans get scared, they open fire.

It's not that Bigfoots couldn't fight back if they wanted to. They might not have guns, but Charlie Raymond believes that Bigfoots are highly intelligent, with well-honed survival skills. They're also super agile, with impressive upper-body strength. They can lift and throw basketball-sized rocks to scare off intruders infringing on their territory. The BFRO later checked such rocks and found that they weighed up to 240 pounds.

On one occasion, Barton Nunnelly's family was awakened around midnight by a thunderous crashing sound that shook the house. At first, they thought a car had plowed into the house. What they discovered, though, was that the garage door had been ripped off its metal tracks by something superhuman, and the door was left lying on the floor. Oddly enough, the dogs didn't bark at any intruder.[15] Nunnelly cites several other instances of Bigfoots lifting cars and even mobile homes—with the occupants still in them. In 1980 one camper at Big Bone Lick State Historic Site in Boone County shot at a Squatch trying to overturn his trailer. The Squatch reportedly took off running, leaped into the Ohio River, and swam away.

To be on the safe side, if you ever encounter a Sasquatch, the BFRO website recommends averting your eyes. Don't stare. The Squatch might interpret this as a sign of aggression. Sit on the ground, which is a nonthreatening move. Scratch yourself. Chew on anything within reach. Groom your companion if you're not alone (that's something Bigfoots apparently do for each other).[16] Raymond also recommends raising your hands, as if signaling "Don't shoot." The next sound you hear is likely to be hysterical laughter from your fellow campers watching you imitate a chimpanzee. But all joking aside, a Bigfoot encounter can be terrifying, despite the apparent lack of aggressive or threatening behavior from Squatches.

If he lived closer to their habitat, Raymond would try to earn the Squatches' trust by going to the same place around the same time, wearing the same clothes, engaging in normal activities such as cooking or playing music to attract their attention, and leaving gifts of food and shiny objects for them. However, Raymond won't reveal where these places are because he doesn't want anyone hunting the creatures or knocking on trees—their supposed form of communication—to invite them over.

Researchers have argued that Bigfoots should be considered an endangered species. In fact, according to *National Geographic*, "Skamania County, Washington, considers itself a Bigfoot refuge, and a 1984 ordinance states that killing this 'endangered' ape-like creature can get you a year in jail, a $1,000 fine or both."[17] If they are not recognized and protected, Charlie Raymond fears that Bigfoots could become extinct in the next hundred years. That's why Kentucky's BFRO is gathering data about credible sightings and migration patterns to better understand the creatures. Deforestation, logging, mining, and urban sprawl have damaged and limited the Squatches' habitat, making it difficult for them to move around or find mates. Pretty soon, Raymond says, they'll have nowhere to go and not enough food to eat. He hopes to gather enough evidence to convince Kentucky to establish laws to preserve land where Bigfoots can survive and thrive.

Sasquatches are not among the 1,442 species listed by the Kentucky Department of Fish and Wildlife as a known species in the state.[18] So where does that leave us? Are the witnesses imagining their encounters? Have scientists studying the biology of Kentucky overlooked something this large and smelly? Are Bigfoot encounters all hoaxes? Like sightings of UFOs or ghosts, many witnesses seem sincere, and we respect their integrity in reporting what they truly believe they saw. Still, that doesn't necessarily mean they encountered a real flesh-and-blood animal.

Many Native American nations share stories about "Old People of the Forest," creatures that are highly intelligent but best avoided. Interestingly, one never sees Native people howling in the woods or knocking on tree trunks to communicate with Squatches. A tribal elder is likely to say that there are things in the wilderness that humans don't understand, and since we don't understand them, we should leave them alone. Ancient Native peoples never read *Moby Dick*, but they knew intuitively that searching for certain white whales was a really bad idea.

Humans create reality out of images, ideas, and narratives stored deep in our memories. What if modern humans are preprogrammed to see big, hairy creatures lurking in the woods? When we encounter a Squatch-like shadow that takes on a humanoid shape, our minds fill in the details and we "see" a Sasquatch because for tens of thousands of years our ancestors shared northern Africa, the Middle East, and Europe with a competing race of strong, hairy, smelly bipeds—the Neanderthals. This is pure speculation, but people of European origin do seem to retain cultural memories of living next to nonhuman "people." European folklore is heavily populated with fairies and gnomes that may look like us and live in the woods near us but that act in strangely different ways. Of course, Neanderthals have been extinct for at least forty thousand years, so there's no reason to fear them *now*—until we hear a deep howl in the woods just beyond the light of our campfire.

VICIOUS MAN-WOLF STALKS LAND BETWEEN THE LAKES

There have been dozens of reports of a man-wolf creature prowling around Kentucky and the Midwest since the mid-1990s. We've combined the details of some of those sightings to come up with this representative tale: Late one night, a couple is driving along a secluded western Kentucky highway near Land Between the Lakes. As they round a bend, their headlights reflect a large animal crouched on the side of the road. "Looks like a big dog," the driver says. But as they draw nearer, the four-footed creature stands up on its hind legs, towering at about seven feet tall. It's holding some sort of roadkill in its two hands (yes, *hands*). Enraged by the intrusion, the creature pricks up its pointed ears, snarls through a wolf-like snout, and bounds into the darkness on two legs. The car screeches to a stop while the couple calls local police to report their encounter. Officers respond, but no evidence of the man-wolf is ever found.

What's going on here? The man-wolf, sometimes called a dogman, cannot exist, and yet, such sightings are common in Wisconsin and Michigan. Witnesses have also reported man-wolves in Kentucky, mainly in two areas: Land Between the Lakes and eastern Kentucky's Red River Gorge in the Daniel Boone National Forest. Descriptions of these creatures are similar: They have canine features, glowing yellow or red eyes, and silver-gray fur. They stand seven to eight feet tall on two legs and have two hands with vicious claws. And they stink. These nocturnal beasts have been seen leaping over cars and ten-foot fences, so they would probably win a footrace against a human.

Man-wolves can also be aggressive. Their massive, crushing jaws and fangs suggest that they can mutilate their prey. They also reportedly growl, howl, or wail, making unearthly sounds that would scare even the most experienced outdoor enthusiasts. If that's not frightening enough, witnesses say the man-wolves don't just stalk the woods hunting deer (or eating roadkill). They sometimes wander over to houses and scratch at the back doors. They've been accused of killing dogs, pigs, goats, and chickens on farms. And, as a final insult, they've been known to chase unsuspecting residents out for an evening stroll. Witnesses are terrified, and they're apparently sincere. So what could these wolf-like creatures be? An actual wolf? A feral dog? A *tulpa*, or a thought-form projected into reality? Or are they all hoaxes?

Kentucky doesn't have a breeding population of wolves, according to the US Forest Service, which lists the gray wolf (*Canis lupus*) as extirpated in the state.[1] However, in March 2024 a hunter shot a large dog-like creature near Munfordville that was at least twice the size of a coyote. According to a report from the Timber Wolf Information Network: "A DNA analysis performed by the U.S. Department of Agriculture's National Wildlife Research Center in Colorado determined the 73-pound animal was a federally endangered gray wolf with a genetic makeup resembling wolves native to the Great Lakes Region. The U.S. Fish and Wildlife Service Forensics Laboratory in Oregon confirmed the finding. How the wolf found its way to a Munfordville hayfield at daybreak in March remains a mystery. Wolves have been gone from the state since the mid-1800s."[2]

This creature was a known species outside of its normal range, not some weird human-canine hybrid or werewolf. This suggests that other reports may in fact be sightings of gray wolves. But most reports include characteristics that do not apply to wolves, such as a bipedal gait, no visible tail, and prehensile front paws—more like a werewolf than a gray wolf. However, these man-wolves, or dogmen, aren't werewolves in the classic sense because the sightings don't correlate with moon cycles and the creatures apparently don't transform from human to canine.

But there's little doubt that some menacing creature is frightening campers and tourists in Kentucky. Our primary case study is a report that has circulated on the internet for years about students from Murray State University (MSU) on a field trip to Land Between the Lakes (LBL) sometime around 1973. According to the story, one spring some MSU biology majors entered LBL to inventory the animal life there. After a busy day collecting data, the students returned to camp by dusk and got a fire going. A male student left camp briefly to use nature's bathroom and returned highly agitated. He told the professor that something was in the woods watching them. Another student said he had heard something sniffing in the weeds near the camp. Now, everyone was creeped out. The scared MSU students, hyperaware that they were miles from help, listened for any unusual movement in the darkness and scanned the surrounding tree line for potentially dangerous intruders. They heard heavy footsteps, followed by some dog-like snuffling in the bushes.

In Ron Coffey's book *Kentucky Cryptids*, a witness suggests that the culprit putting these MSU students on edge was probably a wild hog, which is a good guess.[3] The US Forest Service (part of the US Department of Agriculture), which administers the Land Between the Lakes National Recreation Area, reports that wild hogs are a serious problem in the area. The nonnative animals are feral and destructive. The Kentucky Department of Fish and Wildlife operates a trapping program to reduce the hog population, but hunting them is strictly forbidden.[4] This is how Coffey continues the tale of the creature harassing the Murray State students:

> It seemed to be circling their campsite, moving incredibly swiftly. The campers began to become anxious. They shined their flashlights into the woods in the direction of the footsteps, but saw nothing. And then the howling began. It was a wild, insane howling, like a wolf, only much louder than any wolf could be, and with an unnatural, bloodcurdling quality that made the howling sound almost like mocking laughter. It seemed to come from everywhere around them, first one side of the circle of light around the fire, and then from the other. Soon, the terrified campers began to catch glimpses of a pair of glowing yellow eyes as they ran past in the dark. The terrified campers retreated into their Volkswagen bus, and wisely decided not to stick around to get a better view.[5]

The students sped back toward campus with a "massive, shadowy figure racing behind them, barely visible in the bus's taillights," Coffey writes. In some versions of this story, the "man-wolf" chases the vehicle on two legs. Try as they might, the students can't outrun the mysterious menace. It allegedly grabs one of the vehicle's rear hatches with human-like hands or claws. The petrified driver guns the engine, and the horrified students and their equally panicked professor escape in a cloud of exhaust, returning to the college shaken but safe. When they survey the damage to the VW, they find deep claw marks on the vehicle.

Inquiries about the authenticity of this encounter, made to MSU's Department of Biology, its Public Information Office, and the campus newspaper, have all gone unanswered. The silence might be nothing more than institutional weariness over an old internet tale. But out of professional courtesy, a response would have been welcome. Conspiracy theorists would say the deafening silence just adds to the mystery.

We visited LBL during spring break 2022 as part of our research for this book. But we weren't brave (or foolish) enough to venture into the woods at night to see what might be prowling about. Luckily for us, no man-wolves attacked us at Kenlake State Resort Park. Because our tracking skills are sorely lacking, we knew that finding the elusive creature would be a challenge even in the daytime. Wildlife abounds. For example, park literature indicates that LBL provides refuge to more than 240 species of birds. Dozens of bigger animals are roaming around, but the only huge carnivorous animal mentioned on the state Fish and Wildlife website is the mountain lion, which was declared extinct in Kentucky in 2011: "Currently the nearest wild population of mountain lions resides in Nebraska, more than 900 miles from Kentucky." That would be quite a trek, even on four feet. Coyotes, however, are common in many Kentucky counties. And yet the dozens of Kentucky reports cataloged by Ron Coffey, Linda Godfrey, Luke Penton, and other man-wolf researchers describe an all-too-real and ferocious human-canine hybrid.

We wondered whether the beast spotted in LBL may be a psychological mirage—a subconscious wolf image projected onto a real animal such as a wild hog. We've all had "memories" of wolves implanted into our minds by hours of scary nighttime stories. Remember the Big Bad Wolf? Are people seeing giant wolves in the woods because they're *programmed* to see these creatures in those places? Our ancestors spent centuries living near—and profoundly fearing—actual wolves. Generations later, is there something inside us that tells us to watch for wolves skulking in the shadows? And why do we still remind our children about this danger over and over at bedtime?

As any stage magician can testify, we see what we have been trained to see, what we expect to see, and what our brains are telling us we see. So this isn't necessarily a perception error. If these images are deeply ingrained in our subconscious, the people who report seeing a man-wolf in the woods are in fact "seeing" that image—at least according to their brains. They are not hoaxing or lying. In fact, they would probably pass a polygraph test. But what the brain tells them they're seeing may not be what's actually in front of them.

A new and much more detailed report recently surfaced from Martin Groves, a retired sheriff's deputy from Robertson County, Tennessee. Groves was interviewed by Josh Turner on his *Paranormal Round Table* podcast in August 2022 and by Seth Breedlove for his 2022 documentary *American Werewolves.*[6] At Turner's Dogman/Cryptid Conference that same month,

Groves spoke publicly for the first time about a frightening encounter he had thirty years ago. According to Groves, a pack of man-wolves stalked him and a hunting partner in 1993 and then attacked them. Groves and his friend fired their weapons at the creatures, with no visible effect, so the hunters fled their campsite. When Groves returned the next day to collect his abandoned gear, he was told by park rangers that a search was under way for a bear with mange that might have hurt another hunter who had disappeared without a trace. But no bear was captured, and there was no mention of a lost hunter in local newspapers. In this case, we have an identified witness who is a lifelong outdoorsman familiar with wildlife in the area and some concrete actions not related to a folk story. Still, we have no physical evidence to prove what kind of creature attacked the men.

During our visit to LBL we got the sense that this area is different—set apart—from other places we've been. And, of course, it is physically set apart between the Cumberland and Tennessee Rivers. Folklorists make much of *liminal spaces*—in-between spaces a traveler must enter or cross. When travelers cross into LBL, they find it untamed, magical, and increasingly perilous. In this space, there are no houses, gas stations, or Walmarts. When you cross over into the Land Between the Lakes, you're *someplace else*, a place where magical tales seem real.

Folklorists Martha C. Sims and Martine Stephens have described the act of storytelling as a sacred ritual, what they call the "liturgy of the campfire." And the function of the ritual is the creation of a liminal space:

> The nature of ritual, the way it is framed as a separate time and experience outside the everyday world, allows the participants to enter a space that is different from their real-world environment. By "carving out" that moment from other moments, it can be transformed into something different. Through altering their clothing, language, behavior, etc. (at least in high context rituals), the participants create a liminal space. "Liminality" comes from the word "limen," which means "on the threshold." When we experience a liminal state or are in a liminal space, we are on the edge of something new, a transitional place and time where what we were (our role or status before the ritual began) and what we will be after the ritual ends are mixed and blended; or, in another way of thinking about it, we are neither what we were nor what we will be. For the duration of the ritual, the participants can change identity, become something other than what they typically are. Experiences are heightened,

sometimes aided by consumption of special, perhaps intoxicating, foods or other substances.[7]

By engaging in a "liturgy of the campfire," especially in a liminal area like the Land Between the Lakes, we affirm the place's special status. LBL is the perfect setting for stories that invoke a sense of mystery and danger because it's separate from our familiar environment.

Some researchers have argued that the strange occurrences at LBL may be related to the 270 family cemeteries on the property—the remains of the small communities that once dotted the region. According to the Forest Service website, the recreation area is between one and nine miles wide and more than forty miles long—or 170,000 acres. This works out to about one cemetery per square mile. And these are only the known, marked graveyards of European settlers.

Linda Godfrey, author of several works about cryptids in the Midwest, argues for a strong correlation between man-wolf sightings and graveyards—especially Native American burial sites. In Kentucky, ancient Adena Culture burial mounds were often plundered by settlers searching for artifacts to sell. Even today, these archaeological sites have to be protected by laws; otherwise, people would dig them up, looking for spear points and pottery. Godfrey suggests that some wolf creatures might be the spirit guardians of those ancient sites—their rise triggered by violation of the sacred areas they were conjured to protect. The shape-shifting wolf beings of Native legend reportedly have glowing eyes, powerful jaws, and brutal claws—similar to the modern beast. It's possible, too, says Godfrey, that witnesses might be encountering giant flesh-and-blood wolves—a remnant of an as-yet unrecorded population of Ice Age dire wolves. Fossil records indicate that dire wolves weighed between 150 and 200 pounds, but they couldn't walk on two legs. Nor did they have hands instead of paws.[8] Also, they became extinct thirteen thousand years ago.

Still, early humans feared a predator's attack—the unseen beast growling from the bushes with its glowing eyes and sharp fangs. And perhaps they passed that fear on to their many-times-great-grandchildren who now camp in Land Between the Lakes. The possibility that ancient ancestors are responsible for such inbred fear has been discussed by psychologists and anthropologists as examples of racial or tribal memory. The American Psychological Association's online dictionary contains this entry for "racial memory": "Thought patterns, feelings, and traces of experiences held to be transmitted from generation to generation and to have an influence on individual minds and behavior. Carl

Jung and Sigmund Freud both embraced the concept of a phylogenetic heritage. . . . Jung cited images, symbols, and personifications that spontaneously appear in different cultures, which he explained in terms of the archetypes of the collective unconscious. Also called racial unconscious."[9] Even if such archetypes aren't genetically coded into our brains, popular culture mirrors our deepest fears. For example, Nora Sayer, among others, has argued that the classic 1956 movie *Invasion of the Body Snatchers* reflects a real fear of Soviet spies infiltrating American society.[10] We tell tales (and make movies) about the things we fear most.

Here's an example from popular culture: The horror tale known as "The Hook" has been told in hushed tones at slumber parties for decades. As the story goes, a young couple's romantic evening on Lovers' Lane is interrupted by a radio bulletin about an escaped mental patient who has a hook for a right hand. Soon after the warning is broadcast, the lovers hear a noise in the bushes and see something moving behind the car. In some versions, the boy gets out to investigate and doesn't come back. The quick-thinking girl jumps into the driver's seat and rushes back to town to get help. When she gets to the police station, she finds—wait for it!—a bloody hook dangling from the rear door handle. This motif of the escaped mental patient as antagonist often shows up in fiction (think generic teen slasher movies or Batman's nemesis the Joker, who escapes from Arkham Asylum to wreak havoc on the citizens of Gotham). Perhaps it's because we fear the mentally ill, many of whom are unhoused and untreated. Similarly, perhaps fictional works about zombies are so popular because zombies personify the stereotypes of people experiencing drug addiction. The zombie motif addresses a real and very visible threat to public safety.

On a lighter note, shortly before his death in 1996, we heard Appalachian scholar and poet Jim Wayne Miller read his story "After Twenty Years" to an audience at Berea College. Miller combined "The Hook" with about ten other urban legends in a humorous riff. Miller's opening provides an idea of the story's flavor:

> Somehow my hook got caught in the damn doorhandle. Those kids were playing the car radio so loud, when they spun out from under the trees, and headed back toward town, they couldn't hear me hollering. I almost bled to death. Now I live in another town. I've changed my name from Haken to Stumpf and have a state-of-the-art prosthesis. And even though I'm principal of the high school, when kids pull up beside me at a traffic

> light, their whole car jumping with loud music, or some smart-ass DJ's patter, I still want to get out right there in the street, jerk open their car door, and choke them till they turn blue.[11]

Ultimately, strange creatures prowl some of the murkiest parts of Kentucky—maybe not in the woods as much as in our minds. And that's a dangerous place to be, especially after dark.

DEVIOUS GOATMAN LURES VICTIMS ONTO COAL TRAIN TRESTLE

On May 26, 2019, a ghastly beast that lurks along Pope Lick Creek in eastern Jefferson County claimed another victim, the latest in a grim spree that spans decades. Wait. What? People have actually died in Louisville from a monster attack? Yes—if you believe the harrowing tales of the Goatman, a grotesque half-man, half-goat creature (also called the Pope Lick Monster) that reportedly haunts the Norfolk Southern Railroad trestle bridge inside the four hundred–acre Parklands of Floyds Fork.

Adventurous youths, foolish college students, and impressionable adults are enticed to climb the hundred-foot-high trestle to catch sight of the terrifying creature. This is an active trestle with regular train traffic and no pedestrian pathway, so trespassers must walk along the single track. In 2019 the *Louisville Courier-Journal* reported that the latest victims, fifteen-year-old Savanna Bright and her friend Kaylee, were snapping pictures while walking across the 772-foot-long trestle when a freight train caught them by surprise. Bright was struck and killed. Kaylee fell and sustained serious injuries.[1]

One could argue that the Goatman's prey are harmed by *trains* and not by the monster himself. However, it's clear that the thrill seekers are lured to the trestle by the mystique surrounding the infamous brute. Most victims would have no reason to be on the trestle if not for the Goatman. Authorities haven't kept count of the Goatman's victims, but in 2016 the *Courier-Journal* interviewed retired train engineer Wayne Gentry, who regularly drove that route. During his thirty-four-year career with the railroad, Gentry was involved in forty-three collisions with people on the trestle, only one of whom committed suicide.[2]

Stories told over several generations indicate that the Goatman has claimed dozens of lives. Other victims have suffered terrible injuries, not to mention unbearable trauma. Even with unsubstantiated, anecdotal statistics like these, the menacing creature "has the tragic distinction of being the most dangerous mythical animal in North America."[3] Certainly, he's the deadliest of Kentucky's reported cryptids. As far as we know, the commonwealth's collection of ghosts, UFOs, Bigfoots, lake monsters, and man-wolves have claimed no victims whatsoever.

To be clear, the Goatman poses no danger to the general public—*if* they obey the law. Thrill seekers don't find themselves on the treacherous trestle by accident. To get there, one has to climb over a high fence, scramble up a steep hill, ignore prominent "No Trespassing" signs, and walk out on the narrow, single-track trestle. There are plenty of warnings to "Keep Out."

Among the disheartening Goatman-related cases is one involving an Ohio couple whose search for the supernatural turned into a deadly nightmare. On April 23, 2016, twenty-six-year-old Roquel Bain and her boyfriend, forty-one-year-old David Knee, drove to Waverly Hills, the abandoned and allegedly haunted tuberculosis hospital discussed in an earlier chapter. To kill time until their evening tour, the couple chose to climb the Pope Lick trestle to look for the Goatman. Neither expected to encounter a train on the tracks, especially one traveling straight toward them at thirty to fifty miles per hour. They realized the danger too late to take evasive action. Bain was struck by the train and fell to her death.[4]

Beth Warren, writing in the *Courier-Journal*, interviewed Knee, who narrowly escaped the same fate. "We looked up, and it [the train] was right there, about 40 feet in front of us coming full blast," Knee said. "It's a nightmare waking up each day and realizing it's not a dream." Knee, a weightlifter, managed to hold on to the vibrating trestle until the train had passed, "clinging to the trestle's side with his arms and wrapping one leg around a metal support," Warren writes. "When the train stopped, Knee pulled himself off the ledge and back onto the tracks. He waited between two train cars until the engineer backed the train up so he could safely walk off the bridge."[5]

What were they thinking? you might ask. How could they be so foolish? Before passing judgment, let's look more closely at the Goatman's appeal. What causes seemingly sane people to risk their lives to investigate the beast?

There are several versions of the Goatman legend. Take your pick. In one, the anonymous "they" say it was a dark and stormy night when a circus train, crossing Norfolk Southern Railway's Pope Lick trestle near Louisville, derailed. One survivor couldn't believe his luck. He was part of a freak show and had been beaten, starved, caged, ridiculed, and shunned for his appalling appearance caused by birth defects. The train wreck gave him a chance to escape the torture he had endured for most of his life.[6] So off he went. But he didn't go far. He allegedly made his home in the woods or in a hidden cave under the bridge. And before long, he started seeking revenge on humankind by luring visitors onto the tracks.[7]

Steve Rush's 1990 article in the *New Voice* suggests several possibilities. The Goatman could be a chemist horribly injured by an explosion in his lab, a local farmer's reclusive son who wanders only at night because of his shocking appearance, or even a hermit who lives in a nearby shack and intentionally scares trespassers to protect his privacy.[8]

"They" also say that maybe the monster was a goat farmer who sacrificed his herd to Satan. Author and historian David Domine in Louisville indicates that the farmer got the bad end of the bargain because he was apparently transformed into the very beast he tortured. It seems the farmer, too, seeks vengeance against intruders by terrorizing anyone who dares to walk on the bridge—especially around Halloween or when there's a full moon.[9] Other "theys" claim the creature that sends people to their doom is a Native American skinwalker who's retaliating against settlers who stole his tribe's land.

Whichever legend you choose, be on the lookout for a monster that appears to be a man-goat hybrid with muscular legs and coarse, dark hair all over his body, horns, and cloven hooves. If you don't see the Goatman, you will certainly smell him. Like Bigfoot, he reportedly stinks. In their defense, they probably don't have access to a hot shower for regular bathing and good hygiene.

As if these legends aren't wild enough, a story recorded for Beargrass thunder.com claims that during a full moon, the Goatman's spirit emerges from the dirt and gains power as his body takes shape, giving him the strength to stalk and control his prey. He telepathically probes their minds, hypnotizes them, and orders them onto the dangerous train tracks, where no pedestrian belongs.[10] The helpless victims are paralyzed, powerless to resist his commands. Their energy is zapped. Their eyesight becomes blurry. Their body temperature plummets. If, by some miracle, they do break free, the Goatman will supposedly "reach up and grab your legs and hold you down until the train comes by."[11] There is no way victims can escape. They can only watch helplessly as the train heads toward them at top speed.

If those devious tactics don't work, the Goatman has other tricks to lure his victims onto the tracks. He's a mimic. He can sound like a crying child calling pitifully for Mommy. Who could resist helping a child in distress—even if it means putting one's own life in peril?

Other stories say the Goatman attacks his victims with a blood-stained ax, and either the threat of getting chopped to pieces or the very sight of this repulsive creature prompts some victims to jump off the trestle to escape him. That's a pretty long leap—about one hundred feet down from the eight-story structure. It's nearly impossible to survive such a drop.

So what brings people to the bridge anyway? Some are teenagers making the pilgrimage on a dare. Others are thrill seekers or just plain curious. Some even come more than once. After cheating death the first time, they press their luck. The thrill seekers think they can outrun a train traveling fifty miles per hour and hauling thousands of tons of freight. They can't. No matter how fast people think they are, the odds are against them. The train can't stop quickly enough to avoid hitting pedestrians, and the wooden track makes it hard for runners to maintain their footing. One person got within thirty feet of the end of the trestle before being hit by the train.

There have been other victims, or near victims, as well. For example, thirty-five-year-old James Ratterman died in 1994 while trying to cross the bridge on an all-terrain vehicle. The ATV was not designed to travel on a single-track railroad bridge and overturned—on top of Ratterman. He couldn't free himself in time and was struck by an oncoming train, much to the engineer's horror. Another young man, John K. List, died in 1985 while on the trestle shooting crows with a friend. Certainly there was a safer place to do that.[12]

Some victims climb up to take a picture as proof of their death-defying actions. The picture might survive, but they won't if they misjudge the train schedule. It's hard to gauge when a train might be coming, since the hills and woodlands around the trestle dampen the sound of its approach and hide the train's lights.[13] Out-of-towners might mistake the "rusted and rickety" appearance of the nearly 150-year-old trestle for an abandoned track. But it's still active, with up to twenty-five freight trains rolling through each day. Not great odds for avoiding death—even if you're feeling lucky.

The following cases from the 1990s were reported by Richard Stottman in October 2021 in "Legends of the Deadly Pope Lick Trestle":

- In 1996 one young man survived a near-collision with a train by jumping off the trestle and plunging one hundred feet to the ground. However, a year later he died of the massive injuries sustained in the fall.
- A few trespassers have survived a showdown with trains by dangling over the side of the trestle and hanging on for dear life. One managed a last-second dive to the edge and clung from a cross tie until the train

passed. But it requires herculean strength and stamina to hold on for the five to seven minutes it takes the train to pass. Plus, the speeding train generates colossal vibrations that shake the ground far below, making it almost impossible to get a good grip—and not let go.

- Another quick-thinking fourteen-year-old tucked his body underneath the wooden tracks, which saved his life.
- Back in 1993, six friends were among the fortunate ones who saw a train coming in time. They managed to climb down onto the metal parts of the trestle below the tracks and escape with just minor injuries. However, one girl was too scared to climb all the way down, so firefighters were called to assist. Their ladder, which was "precariously perched on the trestle beams," extended just far enough to make the rescue.

When filmmaker Rod Schildknecht released a sixteen-minute movie, *The Legend of the Pope Lick Monster*, in 1988, critics worried that it might send the wrong message by sparking interest in the Goatman and causing more deaths. But apparently, there is no connection between the movie and subsequent fatalities. Some footage was shot at the bridge site, north of Taylorsville Road and just outside of the Snyder Expressway, but scenes with actors were shot at much safer locations.[14]

Most deaths on the trestle occur at night, when it's hard for the engineer to spot the trespassers in time. But even a warning blast of the horn might not give interlopers enough time to get out of the way. Such senseless tragedies are traumatic for the engineer and for the victims' families. Friends of one young victim spray-painted a message on the trestle, saying that they "love and miss" him. Those close to 2019 victim Savanna Bright left a collage of pictures of her, along with flowers and a sign saying, "Savanna, your wings were ready but our hearts were not."

The railroad has done everything possible to keep people off its private property. Officials erected an eight-foot fence, with chains and bolts. They removed platforms on the bridge to discourage people from walking on it. They posted signs that say "Keep Out," "No Trespassing," and "Danger, Active Train Trestle, Stay Safe, Keep Clear." And they have threatened to levy hefty fines, prosecute violators, and send them to jail.

WDBR.com quotes locals as saying the stakes are too high to risk walking on the trestle. The consensus is, even "if you succeed, you're just a living idiot, you don't prove any points."[15]

Various groups have attacked the problem in other ways. The Parklands of Floyds Fork bought the surrounding land and created a walking path under the trestle that connects the park to other outdoorsy spots. There's even a haunted hike called Legend at Pope Lick. Also, there's talk of erecting a monument or statue of the Pope Lick Monster along the trail. This would give visitors a safer photo opportunity than the trestle itself.

Overall, the legend of the Pope Lick Monster reminds us of the stories told at middle-school sleepovers. No public record has been found of a circus train wreck on the trestle near Louisville. Nor have any birth records surfaced of a baby that looks like a goat. But before we dismiss this legend as mere hijinks, let's think about the Kentucky Goatman in the context of similar tales. The Goatman's identifying characteristics include (1) being humanoid but hideously changed in some way (e.g., horns, hooves), (2) living under or near a bridge in a remote area, and (3) luring unsuspecting folks out onto its bridge and to their deaths. Sound familiar? It should. We've encountered these creatures in many children's books and fantasy stories. That's right. What we have here is a troll. The entry for "troll" in Brown and Rosenberg's *Encyclopedia of Folklore and Literature* begins:

> In Scandinavian folk narrative, trolls are creatures who are usually depicted as gigantic, malicious, dull-witted, ugly, deformed, or animal-like in appearance. Trolls eat or enslave people who wander into their mountainous territory, but those who manage to outwit trolls stand to acquire the treasure—gold or jewels—that trolls hoard. Trolls are particularly antagonistic to Christianity, as is shown in legends about ministers or churches attacked by trolls. Trolls are sometimes depicted as possessing skill as spinners, weavers, or smiths, and they are attracted to beautiful objects and people. Trolls shun the sun and can be destroyed—turned to stone or burst apart—when sunlight hits them.[16]

The association between trolls and bridges seems to be a modern adaptation of the troll motif, appearing in fairy tales such as "The Three Billy Goats Gruff." It even shows up in children's television shows such as *Dora the Explorer*.

A light-sensitive troll might find the area under a bridge attractive, as it provides more or less permanent shade. In a similar way, bridges can provide shelter for homeless persons, so the potential danger posed by mentally ill or criminally minded humans might explain the origins of the bridge-haunting troll. Many such motifs identify real danger—dark woods, deep lakes, abandoned houses, large animals—but disguise the danger's specific agent with elaborate narrative embroidery.

Yet bridges are also seen as points of connection between different regions—the two sides of a creek, for example. Early peoples believed that such in-between (liminal) spaces concentrated the earth's magic. In contrast, these spaces can also be seen as points of separation. Walls around a cemetery, for example, separate the region of the dead from the region of the living. In the United States, bridges might symbolize the dividing line between areas where white people lived and those places where the Racial Other lived.

Writing in *Haunted Bridges*, Rich Newman says: "The truth is that sometimes things do, indeed, go bump in the night, and sometimes those things aren't necessarily supernatural. Tales [of supernatural occurrences near bridges] can also remind us of the ugly elements of humankind—the horrors of war, love stories gone awry, and the malicious things that people can do. The world can be a terrifying place, and these incidents are the foundations for a lot of terrifying stories."[17] Newman lists a number of haunted bridges in the South, for example, that are believed to be where Black men were lynched. Some of these tales are set before the Civil War and involve enslaved persons, but many of these murders occurred well into the twentieth century.

Folk memory works in funny ways. Residents of an area where a race-based lynching took place might remember the crime and many of its details but *misremember* who was responsible for the act. After all, the lynch mob might have included their own grandfathers. So the violence, the drama, and the fear are recalled, but the details are sanitized by the narrative structure of a "haunt." By moving a real-life crime into a supernatural setting, the storyteller makes sure the tale can never be tied to a specific murder and that the perpetrators can never be named, arrested, or punished. In other words, the troll's "Get off my bridge" might have sounded more like "We don't want your kind around here" in real life. And those sentiments can be just as frightening as spying a horrifying half-man, half-goat creature when you're alone at night surrounded by strange sounds.

WATER MONSTERS

Odd Creatures in Lake Herrington and Kentucky Rivers

One clear summer day in the early 1960s, when Mason was about nine, his parents took him and his younger sister, Martha, fishing at Lake Malone State Park in western Kentucky. The 788-acre lake, created in 1961, provided a peaceful setting for a fun family outing. Their father had bought the kids toy fishing rods at a nearby gift shop. The kits included rods, reels, weights, and small red bobbers, but no hooks or bait. That meant no painful hook accidents or grisly struggles to attach live squirming bait to the hooks. It also guaranteed that no fish would be caught that day (clever dad). The parents could enjoy a pleasant afternoon navigating the rented boat around the lake, looking for likely "fishing spots," in total confidence that they wouldn't have to kill, clean, and cook any catch of the day.

While casting and watching their bobbers float, the kids noticed that a big aquatic lake dweller was following the boat. It was hard to miss. "We could clearly see a large silver shape which seemed to lie about five or six feet below us. It was huge," Mason recalls. "The shape—always bright, but ill-defined—moved when the boat moved, and it stopped when we cut the engine." The mystery fish's size and behavior were starting to freak out the kids, but Dad cavalierly suggested, "Drop your line in. Maybe you'll catch it." But, as Mason remembers, "We were more worried about the creature catching us." However, their parents remained unconcerned about any potential threat to the family's safety. "It's just a shadow from the boat," their mother assured them. That relieved Mason—a little. "Well, the sun *was* bright that day. The lake water was reasonably clear. And the boat's aluminum hull was exceptionally shiny. So, it *could* have been a reflection."

Still, the kids weren't completely convinced that they were imagining the creature that was following them. "We spent most of the afternoon looking over the side of the boat as the flickering shape—at least ten feet long—hovered just below us. Always there. But never identifiable." To this day, Mason and Martha believe they were stalked by a genuine lake monster. Their practical parents, however, always insisted that the "monster" was only an illusion created by light being transmitted, refracted, and reflected through the lake water.

"This was one of my earliest experiences with *debunkers*," Mason says. "A reflection? Seriously? We knew we had witnessed something much more mystical with our own eyes." Mason was relieved when it was time to return to the dock. It might seem silly to be frightened by a fish—even a humongous one—but "I felt like prey, and our underwater nemesis was waiting for just the right moment to reach into the boat and grab me and swallow me whole."

The kids never begged to go fishing again—at Lake Malone or anywhere else. But don't judge them for having overactive imaginations. "Remember, we're boomers who were raised at the height of the Cold War when all Americans—children included—thought we might be killed at any moment in a nuclear holocaust." Anxiety prone or not, the Smith kids were hardly the only people to report lake monsters in Kentucky, although other encounters might have been less stressful.

In 1972 Lawrence S. Thompson, a professor at the University of Kentucky, reported seeing a pig-snouted creature with the body of an eel swimming in Lake Herrington, twenty-five miles south of Lexington.[1] Thompson told the *Louisville Courier-Journal* that while at his lake house he spotted the creature several times in the early morning, usually when he was fishing between Chenault Bridge and Wells Landing. All he could see was its pig-like snout sticking up out of the water, followed by a fifteen- to twenty-foot curly tail. It swam quite fast, he said, about the speed of a boat with a trolling motor attached. Although the creature was unlike anything Thompson had encountered in the lake, he wasn't afraid of it. He told the newspaper's Joe Ward that it seemed "shy," and there was nothing threatening or monster-like about it. "It's only a monster in the sense that you'd call an alligator or a crocodile a monster if no one else had ever seen one."[2]

Thirty-five-mile-long Lake Herrington is the deepest lake in Kentucky—249 feet near Dix Dam, with a mean depth of 78 feet. Kentucky Utilities built the dam across the Dix River in the 1920s to provide water for its hydroelectric generating station and to reduce flooding along the Kentucky River. It was quite an "engineering marvel" for its time, according to the nonprofit Herrington Lake Conservation League. Today the 2,335-acre human-made lake located in Mercer, Garrard, and Boyle Counties attracts boaters and fishers, as it's stocked with bluegill, crappie, and three kinds of bass—large, spotted, and white. Outdoor journalist Art Lander says it's also populated with longnose gar, which is common in Kentucky. Lander reminds us that this fish has "an extremely long, narrow snout, and jaws with long, sharp teeth."[3] They can grow bigger than three feet long, with a trophy-sized gar known to reach forty pounds. That would be a hard fish to miss.

So it's not surprising that there are other anecdotal accounts of sightings of unusual creatures in Lake Herrington. A Somerset man who posted on fishin.com in 2007 says his encounter took place during the day, near Chimney Rock. He didn't see the head or tail, but the color and skin texture of his USC (unidentified swimming creature) reminded him of a manatee, only larger—longer than his seventeen-foot boat. And it swam like a whale or dolphin.[4]

Others have reported seeing creatures as big as a school bus or large enough to swallow a VW Bug or a man—whole. Some think it's a giant catfish. A Louisville man, posting on fishin.com in 2007, believes it could be a sturgeon that's grown to "monstrous proportions"—as big as two hundred pounds, which would be nearly impossible to reel in. A woman familiar with Florida bets it's an alligator.

Some speculate on Facebook's Kentucky Unknown site that the creature might be "descended from dinosaurs" that hid in the underground limestone caves that were flooded to create the lake. Trapped once the dam was built, they adapted to live underwater. Since there's so much we don't know about aquatic life, the Facebook chatter claims that a monster might be lurking down there. Perhaps oceans, seas, rivers, and lakes should be our next frontier of exploration.[5]

Lawrence Thompson, who seems to be the most reliable and widely quoted eyewitness of a Lake Herrington creature, was director of the Margaret I. King Library at the University of Kentucky from 1948 to 1963.[6] He also taught Latin, Greek, and Scandinavian languages at UK and maintained a lifelong interest in Kentucky history before passing away in 1986 at age sixty-nine. Because of his background, Thompson was aware of an obscure series of letters written in the early nineteenth century by Constantine Samuel Rafinesque, who held the natural science chair at what was then Transylvania College (now Transylvania University) in Lexington. Rafinesque (1783–1840) published a carefully researched catalog of fish in the Ohio River titled *Ichthyologia Ohioensis*. All of Rafinesque's entries were species he had personally examined. But according to Thompson, in his letters to the American Philosophical Society in Philadelphia, Rafinesque describes a number of exotic species that he saw from a distance but wasn't able to examine. One of these unknown species, Thompson argued, might have been an ancestor of the pig-snouted creature he saw in Lake Herrington. Or, Thompson speculated, the creature might be an ancient but as yet unknown species that swam up the Mississippi and Ohio Rivers millennia ago and somehow escaped notice by modern humans. In support of this theory, Thompson cited the discovery of a living coelacanth, an ancient lobe-finned fish long thought to be extinct, that was captured off South Africa in the 1940s.

In a letter to the *Lexington Herald* dated July 28, 1972, Thompson wrote that until the twentieth century, there were few locks and no dams along the nation's waterways.[7] So it's possible that an unknown fish species could have left the open ocean and swum up the Mississippi, Ohio, Kentucky, and Dix Rivers before entering what is now Lake Herrington. That's quite a trip, and it would take a spunky fish to complete the trek. But with no human-made obstructions at the time, it's plausible. Still, this doesn't explain how even a determined species like that could transition from saltwater to freshwater. And where would something that size find enough food to survive all this time?

If Lawrence Thompson saw a creature with a pig-like snout, a curly tail, and pink skin, we should consider the possibility that he saw an actual pig—or perhaps several pigs—swimming across Lake Herrington. Kentucky's Department of Fish and Wildlife has long struggled to control populations of feral hogs, and a wild hog might look unfamiliar to an observer who isn't used to seeing pigs swim.

Interestingly, Thompson didn't seem the least bit frightened by the creature he encountered, as it wasn't bothering anybody. Confronted with the unknown, Thompson said the only thing a person can do is "ask others to look for the same thing and see what you find."[8] Unfortunately, over the past fifty years, only a few people have officially reported seeing anything like what Thompson witnessed.

While researching his 2015 book *Kentucky's Herrington Lake Monster*, George Dudding found that although many residents knew the local legend, very few had reported actually seeing the creature, which had a variety of names: Underwater Pig, Giant Eel Pig, Herry, Underwater Bigfoot, and the Herrington Lake Monster.[9] Herry might have cousins in other Kentucky lakes and rivers.

A high school friend of Mason's who is an avid scuba diver told us about a "monster" encountered during the recovery of a truck from the Green River near Kincheloe's Bluff at South Carrollton. The Muhlenberg County Sheriff's

Department had hired a diver from Owensboro to locate the submerged truck. In due time, the man arrived, put on his gear, and descended into the nearly opaque waters of the appropriately named Green River. After feeling his way around in the near darkness for a while, the diver finally located a large, cold, silver object about the size of the missing pickup. Keeping one hand on what he believed was the door of the truck, he signaled for more cable so he could attach the tow truck's hooks to the object. At this point, the "truck" suddenly moved, swam away, and vanished. The horrified diver quickly returned to the surface and quit on the spot.

Other stories have circulated for years about giant catfish caught (or almost caught) near Kentucky Dam or Barkley Dam. Apparently, these fish weighed more than two hundred pounds, exceeded eight to ten feet long, and had mouths big enough to devour a dog or a small child. Of course, any fan of Jeremy Wade's Animal Planet series *River Monsters* knows that the world's fresh waters contain some fearsome beasts, many of them reportedly so large they could hold an adult underwater long enough to drown them. But believing that professional "extreme angler" Jeremy Wade could pull a gigantic predator from the piranha-infested waters of Brazil's Amazon River is very different from accepting that a typical Kentucky sportsperson could pull one from Kentucky Lake.

According to the Kentucky Department of Fish and Wildlife, the largest catfish ever caught in Kentucky was a blue catfish weighing 106.9 pounds, pulled from the Ohio River in 2018. The biggest Green River catch on record is a 97-pound flathead catfish caught in 1956.[10] These are huge fish, to be sure, but hardly the stuff of legends—nothing that would attract national attention or warrant the *River Monsters* crew coming to Kentucky.

Any unexplored place can become the stage for mysterious sightings. Like the artwork drawn on the edges of medieval maps, people populate such areas with frightful creatures—avatars for the fear generated by vast spaces filled with unfamiliar life-forms. "There be monsters here!" Case in point: the ancient Israelites, who were not seagoing folk, created images of the frightening, thundering sea where Leviathan—the Bible's sea monster—roams. And it's no accident that Hollywood's 1975 thriller *Jaws* was such a blockbuster. The movie poster of the ferocious-looking shark attacking a solitary swimmer invoked a primal fear that still scares viewers today.

Bodies of water don't have to be huge to generate tales of supernatural inhabitants. In their 2006 book *Lake Monster Mysteries*, Benjamin Radford and Joe Nickell point out that many lakes are said to contain "monsters." Based on 1997 research reported in *Fortean Times* and projecting forward, Radford and Nickell suggest that there must be in excess of three hundred monster-infested lakes worldwide. If each of these lakes had a breeding population of monsters, then surely there would be thousands, if not tens of thousands, of lake monsters swimming in our waters. Even if science missed a monster or two—or even an unlikely dozen—it's hard to believe that biologists and fishing enthusiasts could have overlooked the existence of thousands of them, especially as it seems that such creatures inhabit every body of water larger than a puddle.

The realm of lake monsters may not be actual lakes but rather places where the real and the imaginary overlap, a distinction we've made only in the last two or three centuries. According to Radford and Nickell:

> Before the Enlightenment, rumor, mysticism, and superstition were often seen as perfectly valid ways of knowing about the world. Scholars and authorities often wrote about unknown or mythical creatures as if they were confirmed fact. In 1544, for example, Sebastian Munster wrote the popular *Cosmographia Universalis*, which contains vivid descriptions of dragons and basilisks (winged serpents whose gaze—like that of the snake-haired Medusa—could turn men to stone). Swiss naturalist Conrad Gesner, in *Historia Animalium*, described unicorns and winged dragons, as does Pliny the Elder in his *Natural History*.[11]

So it's a common human practice to populate unknown regions with strange and frightening creatures from our imaginations.

Speaking of imaginations, for several summers beginning in 2009 we taught weeklong creative writing classes for middle-school students at area libraries and art and learning centers. Our students gathered each morning and, with the two of us as coaches, plotted and collaboratively wrote a short story that might involve a Bigfoot, a ghost, or a water creature. In 2009 a group at the Carnegie Center for Literacy and Learning in Lexington chose to write about a lake monster. The sixteen workshop participants crafted a compelling story about a scary monster in Lake Cumberland near Jamestown, Kentucky. Their "solution" to the mystery was that the monster was in fact a Louisiana alligator that had shifted its normal range north because of global warming.

Don't dismiss the idea just because it stems from the imagination of children. It seems entirely possible that Kentuckians could start seeing unusual animals, birds, and amphibians. If climate change is raising temperatures, as research suggests, perhaps tropical species will shift into more northerly environments that they previously found uninhabitable.

Surprise sightings of unexpected (if not exactly unknown) animals can be quite disturbing. If you've never seen an alligator in a local stream, the sudden appearance of this scaly creature would be pretty terrifying. In fact, scholars have suggested that the Leviathan from the Bible (Job 41) is likely a Nile crocodile, an unfamiliar animal to a writer from ancient Israel.

So it's possible that the next time you're out on a Kentucky lake you could encounter a strange aquatic creature swimming alongside your boat—either something completely foreign or perhaps something more familiar doing the pig paddle.

MOTHMAN AND DEMON LEAPER SWOOP AROUND KENTUCKY

One of the creepiest Appalachian legends of all time is the story of Mothman—a huge, car-chasing, leathery-winged creature with claws, sharp teeth, and glowing red eyes that apparently terrorized one hundred witnesses near Point Pleasant, West Virginia, between 1966 and 1967.

Kentuckians could read about Mothman in a November 18, 1966, story from United Press International that appeared on the front page of the *Lexington Leader*: "'Flying Creature' Said Seen along Ohio River." The reporter described "a huge bird-like creature with eyes like 'red reflectors' and a wingspan of 10 feet."[1]

Despite his intimidating appearance, Mothman may have actually tried to warn the tiny town of Point Pleasant about an impending collapse of the Silver Bridge on December 15, 1967, which killed forty-six people. But no one understood his message in time to save the motorists who died. Mothman had been seen perched on the structure at times, but he was not responsible for the bridge catastrophe, which scarred the town for decades. In fact, he never physically harmed anyone, although some suspect he was responsible for several missing dogs. The bridge crumpled because of poor 1920s engineering, lack of maintenance, and overloading. But thanks to some astute marketing, a book by John Keel, and a Hollywood movie starring Richard Gere, Point Pleasant has turned its scary monster and associated bridge tragedy into a tourist attraction, complete with an impressive museum, a giant statue, and a Mothman Festival held in September.

We are among the curiosity seekers who have visited Point Pleasant—twice. We enjoyed conversing with the friendly townspeople while devouring Mothman pizza (with olives for eyes), munching Mothman-shaped cookies (with Red Hots for eyes), and chasing it all down with Mothman root beer, wine, and beer. We even bought T-shirts with Mothman prominently featured. And, like moths to a flame, we were drawn to the seven-foot-tall stainless-steel statue of Mothman erected near the center of town. The statue has a reflective rear end, and tourists like us are urged to "Come see Mothman's shiny hiney!" and rub it for good luck.

Mothman left West Virginia after the bridge collapse, but he didn't disappear entirely. He's been spotted at various places from Chicago to Chernobyl. But has this red-eyed apparition with a shiny bottom ever ventured into Kentucky? Absolutely.

On October 20, 2020, Ohio-based documentary filmmaker Seth Breedlove released *The Mothman Legacy*, produced by his video company Small Town Monsters. Erica Bivins of WTVQ-TV in Lexington reported that much of the film was shot in the Bluegrass and deals with Kentucky sightings of the bat-winged creature that is said to be a harbinger of doom. Breedlove said that, for the first time, they had to limit the witness encounters they taped "because there's so many people that have claimed to see Mothman."[2]

What is usually missing is visual proof, although some astute photographers allegedly snapped pictures of Mothman even earlier than 1967. These have been making the rounds on Mothman internet sites for years. First, let's consider two photographs that allegedly show Mothman perched on a suspension bridge. According to one caption (there are several conflicting ones), the photos were taken at Russell, Kentucky, near Ashland in Boyd County, only sixty highway miles and perhaps as few as forty air miles from Point Pleasant. The first photograph, time-stamped November 13, 2003, seems to show a huge bat-like creature crouching on the bridge's superstructure and looking down on the river at twilight. A second image, taken immediately after, shows the creature taking flight with large, leathery wings.[3]

Skeptics point out that the photos' poor quality and inconsistent lighting make it difficult to make out important details. But the figure, which doesn't resemble a bird, a plane, or Superman, does look menacing. The photographers are not identified, but the caption suggests that the photos were taken by a couple who reported seeing the creature's red, glowing eyes from halfway across the river.

The structure in question could be the Oakley Clark Collins Memorial Bridge, which spans the Ohio River from Russell to Ironton, Ohio, and carries thousands of cars every day. The white, cable-stayed bridge opened for traffic on November 23, 2016. Its predecessor, the purple, cantilever Ironton-Russell Bridge, opened in 1922—six years before Point Pleasant's Silver Bridge was built.

So, how can we be sure where this image came from? A Google search turns up several hits—with only some listing the location as Russell, Kentucky, and none of them crediting the photographer. In fact, the same image has been used to illustrate stories about Point Pleasant's bridge and sightings of flying humanoids in other parts of the country, with no attribution. A number of similar images that claim to depict flying humanoids, including some taken in the Chicago area in 2017, have been debunked as a hawk carrying a dead rabbit back to its nest. The dangling, human-like legs are simply the limp body of the hawk's prey seen in silhouette. Anonymous postings with conflicting, sketchy, or no attributions make us suspicious. So the unattributed photo is hardly compelling proof that Mothman invaded Kentucky. Remember, we live in the age of affordable, consumer-friendly graphics programs that any middle-school student can use to float a "realistic" flying saucer or winged cryptid into any standard photo and then print it out. Presto! Close Encounters of the Photoshop Kind. If we ever manage to capture a genuine image of Mothman (or Bigfoot or a flying saucer), we'll copyright the image instantly and sell it to the highest bidder.

By contrast, the testimony of a recent Kentucky eyewitness is more intriguing. Stephanie Hanson posted a comment on Facebook's Kentucky Unknown site describing an encounter she had in November 2021 while driving on Highway 313, headed home to Elizabethtown from her job in Shepherdsville:

> One night I saw something that I thought was a dragon swoop down over my car. It scared me so bad I pulled over to try and figure out what the hell I just saw. I stepped out and could see it flying away back over the forest. I mean it was literally head[ing] right towards Fort Knox. I just recently learned about the Mothman, and I believe in my heart that what I saw was the Mothman. I was so freaked out that night [that] I went home and was telling my family about it. Everyone kept saying it was just a bird, and it [had] just startled me, but I'm telling you this thing had at least a 15-foot wingspan. It was absolutely massive.[4]

Hanson calls herself an avid bird watcher, so she's sure the flying object didn't have any feathers. She described it as dark brown or black with extremely large, leathery, bat-like wings. "I've never seen it again," Hanson said. "Whatever it was, was so close it could have reached out and touched my car. And it was flying faster than I was driving. I was driving 65 miles an hour at the time."

Given Hanson's description, what did she see on that stretch of highway? Skeptic Joe Nickell, interviewed on the *Monster Quest* episode about Mothman, argued that it's extremely hard for eyewitnesses to estimate size accurately when a creature is seen against the open sky with no frame of reference. A large barn owl, for example, might look like a child-sized monster if the witness was frightened, observing it in the dark, and attempting to catch a glimpse of the object through the side window of a moving car.[5]

It's tempting to side with the skeptics on this one. All the large flying creatures that inhabit Kentucky are birds, not huge bats and certainly not dragons. Logically, the witness—if sincere—must have seen an unfamiliar but extremely big bird. And yet Hanson was alert, got a good close-up view of the featherless creature, and didn't try to profit from the encounter. It also caught our attention that the object was flying toward Fort Knox, since many strange encounters occur near military bases. But Hanson was already familiar with Mothman. Could that have clouded her judgment?

Another theory is that Mothman is really a sandhill crane, which has a wingspan of nearly eighty inches. These gray birds have red foreheads and long pointed bills, and their long legs trail behind in flight. But we attended a sandhill crane weekend at Barren River Lake State Resort Park near Glasgow and can rule out cranes. The migrating birds are extremely loud and travel in flocks of hundreds.

So Hanson's Mothman sighting falls into one of those gray areas with no definitive answer. Another report circling the gray area "between day and night, between sight and sound," happened on an August night in 2005 when Jonah Cartwright, a twenty-something factory worker from Florida, was sitting quietly on his back balcony in Louisville. His apartment was in one of the Victorian mansions that line Third Street, along what used to be called Millionaire's Row in Old Louisville. Cartwright was reaching for his empty beer bottle before heading inside for the night when he was startled by a loud whoosh, "like a big bird coming in for a dive." Before he could react, Cartwright said, "a shadow came down out of nowhere and landed on the edge of the roof, just two or three yards away from me. That sight will stay in my head until the day I die. It was something demonic, maybe a mutant or something. I don't know. But it was totally unnatural."[6]

Intrigued by this encounter, Louisville historian David Domine pressed Cartwright for a more detailed description. "It was as tall as me, but completely black. It had wings like a bat, and its legs were very powerful. When it landed in front of me, it kept its wings open most of the time, so I didn't get a good look at its face, but it did seem to have sharp features, from what I could tell. Maybe a pointed chin, something like that. I'm not sure, but it could have had a tail." The intruder stayed for only a few seconds before it hopped to a nearby building and then vanished into the night. "When the thing landed and then took off again, I could hear the scrape of claws or talons on the tarpaper of the roof," Cartwright reported.[7]

Domine notes that Cartwright's apartment was located two blocks away from Louisville's Walnut Street Baptist Church, an imposing, gargoyle-encrusted Gothic building constructed in 1900—over the vocal objections of many residents of Old Louisville. During a 2015 interview for WAVE-TV, Domine said, "People looking up to the spires for a number of generations now have reported sightings of a strange gargoyle-like creature. Some people thought it was one of the Gargoyles on the spires that came to life." This creature is known as Kentucky's Demon Leaper. "It's a bat-like creature with leathery skin, wings, and claws and talons, and it's been seen to hop along the roof," Domine said.[8]

The Demon Leaper hasn't limited its appearances to the church. It has also been seen leaping on and off houses throughout the Third Street area. Cartwright's sighting was only one of many that continue to the present day.

Apparently, decades before the Demon Leaper appeared in Louisville, some kind of winged humanoid was reported across the nation, including in Kentucky. The initial sighting came from New York. On September 12, 1880, the *New York Times* ran a story about a creature seen over Coney Island heading into New Jersey. The article, headlined "An Aerial Mystery," stated, "About a month ago [mid-August 1880] an object of precisely the same nature was seen in the air over St. Louis by a number of citizens who happened to be sober, and are believed to be trustworthy. A little later it was seen by various Kentuckians as it flew across the state." The unnamed reporter didn't claim that the flying creature was anything paranormal or unnatural. "It was apparently a man with bat's wings and improved frog's legs," the reporter said. "That this aerial apparition is a man fitted with practicable wings there is no reason to doubt." But why would the builder of such a marvelous device not cash in on his invention by selling tickets? "The reason is obvious. The flying man is engaging in some undertaking which he cannot safely proclaim. In other words, he is an aerial criminal!"[9]

The *New York Times* may be an elite newspaper today, but just because it reported something in 1880 doesn't mean it actually happened. The late nineteenth century was not exactly a high point for American journalism. In fact, the tone of the article suggests that the entire story may be a hoax. But assuming that the newspaper's account is based on a real observation, it's interesting that the reaction was so different from the modern reaction in Louisville. The 1880 observer expresses wonder at a marvelous modern contraption, not fear of a paranormal apparition. Of course, the *Times* is reporting on an object seen at an estimated height of one thousand feet, while Cartwright's encounter was at a range of six to ten feet. Perhaps it's no surprise that the nineteenth-century observer was amused while the twenty-first-century witness was terrified.

Domine cites another close encounter with the Leaper from Third Street. This one occurred sometime in the late 1980s. Marc McConnell, a student at the University of Louisville, was visiting at a friend's apartment. He walked to the window that overlooked a small balcony jutting out from the house and facing the neighboring house—at fairly close quarters. When he was just a foot or two from the window, McConnell saw something swoop down and land right outside. "I saw something in Old Louisville that defies explanation," McConnell told Domine. "It had big wings and claws and it scared the life out of me." The creature stood about six feet tall when fully erect and had large leathery wings, so McConnell was certain the visitor was not a bird. "When I first saw it, my heart just skipped a beat, and my first reaction was that one of the gargoyles from the big church on the corner had come to life. But before I had any more time to study the thing, it jumped up into the air and was gone. As it jumped, I noticed it had feet like a bird's. I could see curved talons as well." The next morning, McConnell and his friend found scratchy impressions about twice the size of his hand.[10]

Domine writes that, to this day, visitors to Old Louisville stop in front of the Walnut Street Baptist Church and stare up at its Gothic roofline, just in case the Leaper is available for a photo opportunity. We understand the anticipation. We've lingered there ourselves on the off chance we might catch a glimpse. Sadly, we've never found him at home.

But if we Kentuckians want to embrace our own homegrown monster and market it to the masses, we propose a Demon Leaper–themed bourbon or perhaps a Demon Leaper stakes race at Keeneland or Churchill Downs to boost our already growing tourism industry. We could even serve Leaper-like pizza and cookies.

CONCLUSION

The Truth Is Out There . . . Somewhere

By now, it should be clear that we suspect UFOs are most likely Uncle Sam and the Brits covertly testing their top-secret flying machines; that Bigfoot, man-wolves, and river monsters are cultural memories of ancient dangers; and that ghosts are often bad plumbing and wooden beams creaking. You might conclude that we're skeptical debunkers. Fair enough. We *are* skeptical about certain claims, as all of us should be. But after visiting many of Kentucky's paranormal sites, we remain open to the possibility of new discoveries. We're continually stunned by the beauty and complexity of the universe. Like Hamlet, we believe that "there are more things in heaven and earth, Horatio, than are dreamt of in your philosophy."

Our world is filled with mysterious occurrences that seem to have no obvious explanation. Delving into these mysteries has led us to fascinating places like the International Paranormal Museum and Research Center in Somerset for background information and the Kelley Community Park's UFO playground. We're tickled that in 2024 Lexington beamed a message into deep space inviting any passing aliens to come visit the Bluegrass State—as long as they promise not to eat us. And then there's Mothman with his shiny hiney.

Believers and skeptics approach these mysteries from different perspectives, either by looking inside the known universe of matter and energy or by searching outside that universe for some undefined dimension. We realize that hoaxers and attention seekers run amok on social media and television, so getting the facts of any given report can be as difficult as proposing a coherent theory to explain it.

Many witnesses, however, appear to be normal, sincere, sober, down-to-earth folks who have seen something strange that they can't explain. They want to describe it as accurately as possible, even if they can't believe their own eyes.

Could they be hoaxers or honestly mistaken? Either one, but what if we're on the verge of a major change in how humans see the world? Fifth-century Saint Augustine of Hippo wrote in *The City of God*, "Miracles occur not in opposition to nature but in opposition to what we know of nature."[1] We still have a lot to learn about the way the world works. Who knows what we might discover?

In the 1950s and 1960s Dr. J. Allen Hynek called encounters with the unknown "high strangeness," which can cause cognitive dissonance (when our attitudes or beliefs are out of sync with our observations) and create existential anxiety. Such anxiety can become crippling because witnesses to paranormal events almost never find satisfying answers to their questions. And all too often they're belittled by family, friends, and their own community. (Remember the three women who recalled being abducted by aliens, and the farm family harassed by "little green men"?)

Most of the people we've interviewed and researched lead normal lives—except for that one moment when they encountered something totally weird. The question is: did that event occur in a physical reality, or did it play out in the theater of the mind? As philosophers and theologians have noted, the answer is difficult to pin down because we experience *every* event in our minds. Can we ever really know whether we're seeing a realistic drama visible to others or a surrealistic nightmare that we alone experience?

Skeptics argue that if witnesses *were* experiencing actual events—such as nuts-and-bolts UFOs or flesh-and-blood cryptids—there would be far more physical evidence. For example, we'd be tripping over Bigfoot bodies and bits of alien technology. None of that has happened. So skeptics argue that paranormal encounters are "real" only in the witnesses' minds. Houses aren't haunted; people are haunted. And indeed, many of the reports shared in this book are personal recollections of a single individual with no physical proof for support.

We believe our witnesses saw something extraordinary—whether it was out of this world or just out of their frame of reference. For any perceived event, paranormal or otherwise, there's always a trigger in the physical environment and the brain's interpretation of that trigger. Unfortunately, the two don't always agree. We'll illustrate this idea with a holiday ghost story. Years ago, Mason drove to his hometown, Central City, to visit his widowed father. "It was right before Christmas," Mason recalls, "and Dad had gone to bed early. I watched TV downstairs for a while before going upstairs to my old bedroom, where I fell asleep." But Mason's "long winter's nap" was about to be interrupted. "About 5:00 a.m., I was awakened by my mother's voice, calling me to breakfast as she'd done every day for my entire childhood," Mason said. However, his mother had passed away several years earlier. "I sat up in bed, eyes open, fully awake, and again heard my mother call, 'Mason, breakfast's ready!' as she had always done—winter, spring, summer, and fall. I dressed (not realizing the early hour) and went down to the cold and still-dark kitchen, only to find everything exactly as Dad and I had left it the night before. I saw no movement, no apparition, and, sadly, no breakfast."

Mason's experience, though explicit, was almost certainly an "interior reality," perhaps triggered by a vivid dream or some exterior sound. His father, who was sleeping downstairs, closer to the kitchen, heard nothing. First, let's consider the setting. The experience occurred while Mason was sleeping in his childhood home, in his childhood bedroom. It was Christmastime, when people think about family, traditions, and deceased loved ones. Also, Mason heard his mother's voice while he was hovering in the gray area between sleep and wakefulness. People in that state often report hypnopompic hallucinations—visions that occur upon waking from sleep—and hypnagogic hallucinations, which occur at the onset of sleep. Plus, Mason and his father had enjoyed a bountiful supper with relatives the previous night, and dreams can be influenced by what one eats before bedtime. So, like Ebenezer Scrooge said to Jacob Marley's ghost, "There's more of gravy than of grave about you, whatever you are." Scrooge believed the apparition was merely a dream prompted by his late-night meal rather than his partner rising from the grave to deliver a message.

And yet, to Mason, the experience *seemed* physically real. "I was sitting up in bed, eyes open, totally alert," he argues. "I know about hypnopompic hallucinations, but to this day I believe I was fully awake, especially when I heard my mom's second call." Did Mason hear an owl or a train whistle or a distant sound from the street that his sleepy brain misinterpreted as his mother's voice? Or was there a different trigger that we haven't considered yet? Is there another level of consciousness—a separate "real" reality that lies somewhere between physical matter and energy and complete fantasy?

"Miracles [experiences that contradict the known laws of nature] are not about titillating hyperphysical acrobatics," said psychologist and philosopher Michael Grosso. "Their importance lies in the fact that they foreshadow a revolution in our understanding of human reality itself."[2] Grosso and his colleagues point to increasing evidence of a level of reality that exists just outside our visual range, and the brain occasionally snaps that shadow reality into focus without warning. Unfortunately, such hypernormal experiences are fleeting and can't be repeated on demand, which is why they're so hard to document and study. But at least a few scholars are arguing that our lives can include occasional encounters with a different realm of reality—often just a glimmering of some unknown manifold of the multiverse.

For example, a few years ago, our guide on a walking tour of Gettysburg, Pennsylvania, told the story of a shop owner who went down to his basement one July afternoon and instead of finding a storeroom filled with merchandise, he discovered a screaming, bloody, chaotic madhouse. In the eerie yellowish lamplight he saw a makeshift Civil War hospital room—with men moaning, surgeons frantically working on patients, and a blood-drenched floor. "Don't just stand there!" shouted one doctor. "We need more bandages and clean water. Now!" The shop owner hurriedly retreated upstairs to fetch the supplies. When he returned, he found only the hauntingly dark and silent storeroom.

Is this an example of the shop owner's imagination running wild? Perhaps. But the building had been used as a dressing station and a field surgery following the bloody Battle of Gettysburg. The fighting on July 1–3, 1863, generated fifty thousand casualties in a town with fewer than ten thousand residents. So nearly *every* building was used to house wounded and dying soldiers. The battle was certainly real, the soldiers' suffering was genuine, and in 1863 there was a dressing station at that exact location. Based on these concrete facts, the witness may have had a "real" experience in his mind.

Michael Grosso, Edward F. Kelly, and Rupert Sheldrake, among others, have espoused the theory of an "unbounded mind." To paraphrase their position: the human mind may be like a radio that tunes into consciousness rather than a broadcast that creates consciousness. These researchers claim that some people may be able to "tune in" to things that occurred before they were born because those memories are stored extracorporeally, shimmering just out of sight in the unbounded mind. According to this theory, the Gettysburg shopkeeper tuned in to a "memory" of a real event when his mind, without warning, snapped into focus, like a patient looking at an eye chart through the optometrist's eye-testing machine (a phoropter) who can suddenly read even the bottom line of tiny letters.

Needless to say, the antimaterialist theories of Grosso, Kelly, and Sheldrake are *highly* controversial. Skeptics point out that no physical, repeatable-in-a-lab evidence exists to support a theory of nonbiological consciousness. They also note that calling an experience "real" but not visible is no different from calling it a vivid hallucination. And what about UFO, ghost, Bigfoot, and man-wolf witnesses? They aren't experiencing echoes of prior events. They're reporting a totally different reality, one populated by cryptids, spirits, monsters, and little green aliens.

Here, we've focused on sincere people reporting their phenomenal experiences. The three Liberty women, for example, said they encountered something anomalous on the road between Stanford and Hustonville. Bart Nunnelly and his family experienced a terrifying animal attack on their home near Henderson. We have no idea what these people actually saw in a physical, material sense. Through their detailed reports, though, we know exactly what they saw in their minds.

Calling such witnesses fantasy-prone individuals or hoaxers doesn't address the question of why they reported their curious experiences. Did that University of Kentucky professor hallucinate a weird creature swimming in Lake Herrington? It's possible. Healthy, high-functioning people sometimes have hallucinations unrelated to mental illness or to drug or alcohol use. Or they could be honestly mistaken about a mundane experience that triggered the seemingly logical thought that there's a peculiar pig-snouted amphibian swimming in the local lake. It's also possible that they are the victims of a hoax, fraud, or scam created to scare or upset them. Then there's the case of our Gettysburg guide's grisly story, which might be a piece of fiction designed to entertain tourists like us. Or did these witnesses encounter something else?

We realize such a suggestion sounds like New Age babble from the 1990s. But before dismissing the idea, remember Antoni van Leeuwenhoek (1632–1723), who built the first microscope in 1676 and single-handedly invented microbiology. Prior to that, no one suspected that microorganisms even existed. But the instant van Leeuwenhoek looked through his homemade lens, an entire ecosystem of unknown life appeared.

Science has often unveiled new worlds that existed all along but remained undetected because they were not only unseen but also unsuspected. To medieval scholars, heaven was just above their heads and hell was just below their feet, until Galileo and Isaac Newton unveiled a massive universe of stars and galaxies. And to early Renaissance naturalists, European animals were the only survivors of Noah's Flood, until fifteenth- and sixteenth-century explorers returned with unknown specimens from Asia, Africa, and America. Early twentieth-century physicists thought they knew all the laws of motion, until Albert Einstein rewrote the books. Who can guess what other unknown realities may exist, perhaps right in front of us? We just need someone to teach us how to see this new reality.

Questions about the *reality* of reality arise in both psychology and philosophy. Do we live mainly in a universe of nuts-and-bolts materials or in a universe created entirely by the mind and consciousness? In our daily lives, we usually assume that the universe is *real*, in the sense of physical stuff being "out there" (outside our brains), and that this real world interacts in ways that Newton would be able to explain.

By contrast, an *ideal* universe might resemble the one Plato describes in his dialogues or, to cite a pop culture reference, the one Neo is fighting to escape in *The Matrix*. In the latter, reality is a montage (a matrix) of images, forms, or impulses fed into our brains that we perceive as reality but may not have a physical existence beyond our thought universe.

Consider how much literature turns on the question of dream versus reality. Did Hamlet really see his father's ghost, or was that only a dream? In *Don Quixote*, is the elderly knight crazy, or does his faith and bravery make him the only sane character in the novel? In *Slaughterhouse Five*, is Billy Pilgrim hallucinating, or is he really time-traveling with aliens from the planet Tralfamadore?

We'll leave this debate to the psychologists and philosophers, who may shed light on how we interpret witness testimony about a hypernormal reality. For example, in what extraordinary way could something be there and yet not *physically* be there? (We mean in a sense other than Gertrude Stein's comment about her hometown of Oakland, California: "There's no *there* there.") If someone sees a Bigfoot in the Daniel Boone National Forest, even though there's no confirmation that a large, bipedal nonhuman exists in Kentucky, the sighting is real to the witness. But if we were standing right next to that person, would it be real to *us*?

If you're a science fiction fan like us, you're familiar with the word "multiverse." Have paranormal witnesses encountered a flickering cross-over from an alternate, transdimensional reality, like the mirror universe in a *Star Trek* episode or the alternate universes that produced three Spidermen in *Spider-Man: No Way Home* (2021)? This is an attractive possibility, but physicists insist that the multiverse, though useful for explaining some contradictions in quantum mechanics, is still largely a mathematical construct lacking substantial physical proof. As far as we know, any crisscrossing between the two universes can happen only at the quantum level.

Still, our brains may store some memories transdimensionally. In February 2022 Mirza Newton posted "Scientists Find a Multidimensional Universe Inside the Human Brain" on physics-astronomy.com. Newton cites a study published in *Frontiers in Computational Neurosciences* that found the human brain can create in, and deal with, up to eleven dimensions.[3]

The solution to all this "high strangeness" may be weirder than we ever imagined. Researcher and author Jerome Clark has spent years studying reports from the files of the Center for UFO Studies. He claims that the "extraterrestrial hypothesis" is only one option, and perhaps not the most engaging one, to explain UFOs. Clark notes that the act of investigating unknown phenomena may open up entirely new models of how the universe operates. Like physicist Max Planck, Clark suggests that consciousness may be one of the elemental components of the universe. Thus, an event taking place inside consciousness would be as "real" as an event occurring inside the matter-energy continuum. In other words, "We cannot easily distinguish where precisely the event phenomenon and its experiential correlate end and begin," Clark says. "We would all be better off if, when the occasion called for it, we pretended to no false authority but instead boldly uttered three one-syllable words seldom heard . . . *We don't know*."[4]

So, if we're looking at some new manifold of reality—a completely different model heretofore undiscovered and undocumented—should we be scared? If history is any guide, the answer is no. As science has moved forward over the centuries, various discoveries have revealed entire new worlds—new universes—for us to explore, each one more wonderful and more mysterious than the last. Van Leeuwenhoek and his microscope, Galileo and his telescope, and Max Planck, Niels Bohr, and Erwin Schrodinger and their quantum equations brought us strange new worlds—astonishing, dazzling, bewildering worlds!

Toward the end of the movie *2001: A Space Odyssey* (1968), when the marooned astronaut Dr. Dave Bowman finally enters the black monolith, one of his final lines is, "My God, it's filled with stars!"[5] His encounter with the numinous is one of beauty, wonder, and elegance. He doesn't understand the new reality, but something within that reality cared for him and kept him alive. It had been there all along, watching, waiting, nurturing.

Similarly, toward the end of Carl Sagan's novel *Contact* (1985), Dr. Ellie Arroway, played by Jodie Foster in the 1997 movie adaptation, finally reaches the star Vega. She is talking to an alien, who has appeared to her in the form of her long-deceased father. Sagan's fictional first-contact situation is not *War of the Worlds* or *Independence Day* or even *Arrival*. It's a scene in which the young scientist speaks to a much-loved parent:

> "Time to go home," her father said gently.
> It was wrenching. She didn't want to go. . . . She tried asking more questions.
> "How do you mean, 'go home'? You mean we're going to emerge somewhere in the solar system? How will we get down to Earth?"
> "You'll see," he answered. "It'll be interesting."[6]

Interesting indeed! Very few of our witnesses reported any physical injuries from their paranormal encounters. What's out there may be bizarre, but it's apparently not deadly or evil.

If we ever encounter an example of high strangeness—a door into an unknown universe—we suspect the correct reaction will be not terror but amazement. We won't scream or faint or cry. We hope we'll be like Mr. Spock from *Star Trek* and say: "Fascinating!"

EPILOGUE

"The Little Red Hen"

Here's one final Kentucky ghost story. It's our all-time favorite. You'll see why.

Alma Smith, Mason's mother, loved the children's tale "The Little Red Hen." It's about a hardworking hen who wants her friends the fox, the cat, the rooster, and the dog to help her plant and harvest some wheat, mill the grain, and bake a loaf of bread. Her lazy friends, however, refuse to help, so she does all the work herself. When Alma read the Little Golden Book version of the tale to Mason and his sister (often and expressively), she always punched the refrain this way: "Well then, I'll do it my*self*, said the Little Red Hen, and she *did*!" Our own home library contained about a hundred children's books for our four kids, but for some reason, we never had "The Little Red Hen" in our collection of bedtime stories.

One night when our oldest daughter, Ruby Margaret, was a preschooler, she came down with some sort of bug. We tried everything we could think of to comfort her, but nothing worked. She fussed fitfully for hours. She couldn't sleep, so neither could we. Then, suddenly and inexplicably, as if someone had flipped a switch, Ruby stopped whimpering. We heard no more sniffling on the child monitor. It was a relief, but also a puzzlement. We rushed into Ruby's room to check on her and found her lying in bed with her blankets, pillow, and favorite stuffed animals tucked around her. "Are you OK?" we asked.

"Yes," she assured us. "Grandma's here. She's going to read me a bedtime story."

As it happened, both of Ruby's grandmothers had died years earlier. She never knew either one. We glanced around the room. It was empty—at least to our eyes. Perhaps we should have been more alarmed at the news that a long-deceased grandparent had popped in for a visit like Endora from *Bewitched*.

But Ruby seemed perfectly content, and we were extremely sleep deprived, so we gave her a hug and a good-night kiss, checked the closets and under the bed for intruders, and left her in her grandmother's capable, though spectral, hands.

We didn't hear another peep all night. The next morning at breakfast, we asked Ruby Margaret, who was feeling much better, how she got along with her grandmother. "Fine," she said.

"Was it the short woman with gray hair [Marie's mom, Charlotte] or the tall woman with blonde hair [Mason's mother]?" we asked.

"Tall, with blue eyes," Ruby said, describing Mason's mother, whom she had never met.

After the shock wore off, we asked her what story they read.

"The Little Red Hen," Ruby said. "And Grandma really liked one part." She then stood up, put her right hand on her hip, and said enthusiastically, "Well then, I'll do it my*self*, said the Little Red Hen, and she *did*!"

ACKNOWLEDGMENTS

Most of the subjects we write about in this book are dead, legendary, or alien. But many living beings earned our undying gratitude for sharing their fascinating experiences with us. They spared no dramatic details, which made our research more exciting and, we hope, your reading more engaging.

First, thanks to Bill Goodman, former executive director of the Kentucky Humanities Council, who interviewed Mason on his podcast in 2019 about Kentucky ghosts, cryptids, and UFOs. Mason has long believed that ordinary people who report such unusual encounters aren't necessarily seeking fame; they're just trying to make sense of an extraordinary event. Based on the podcast, the University Press of Kentucky invited Mason to write a book about paranormal activity in the commonwealth. Marie, having heard these stories throughout her marriage to Mason (forty-two years) and having collaborated with him on many previous projects, signed on as coauthor.

Editors Ashley Runyon, Alice Fugate Brown, and Natalie O'Neal; Linda Lotz, copyeditor extraordinaire; and the anonymous peer reviewers who recommended publication were enthusiastic about this project. We appreciate their faith in our writing, research, and storytelling and their belief that curious folks like you would buy this book.

As former journalists, we decided to collect material not only through articles, books, and interviews but also by visiting as many sites as possible across the state. We wanted to see for ourselves where these curious sightings and events occurred. We enjoyed these travels immensely for both the insights they provided and the remarkable people we met who supplied us with new, compelling facts.

Although we had thoroughly researched the bizarre story of the little green men who terrorized a farm family near Hopkinsville in 1955, we were in for a delightful surprise when Amy Rogers and Brooke Jung, with the Hopkinsville–Christian County Tourism Office, gave us the coordinates of a life-sized spaceship parked nearby in Kelley Station Park. We're also in Amy and Brooke's debt for directing us to the Pennyroyal Area Museum, where Alissa Keller showed us a display about the impish aliens—with colorful storybook panels that read like a comic book. Alissa also generously shared the museum's impressive files of the event.

WHOP radio in Hopkinsville made a valiant attempt to locate tapes of recorded interviews with witnesses of the 1955 encounter. Sadly, they were gone—disintegrated, taped over, or thrown out.

Our luck improved as we marveled over the knowledge of five exceptional guides and noble guardians of history during our various tours. They have immersed themselves in the history and mystery of their respective historic homes and exhibit an insatiable desire to share these tales with others.

Debra Parrish gave us the grand tour of Liberty Hall in Frankfort—eternal home of the helpful Gray Lady who makes occasional ghostly appearances. Even though we were alone on the tour one dark and stormy afternoon, Debra spared no details about the influential Brown family that once lived there. Best of all, she didn't flinch when the lights flickered once, twice, three times—a spooky start to a tantalizing tour.

Likewise, Stephanie Thurman regaled us with spirited stories about White Hall, the home of abolitionist Cassius Clay. Since it's near our own home in Richmond, we had visited on numerous prior occasions but had never heard about some of the strange occurrences and Stephanie's personal rules for peacefully coexisting with the ghosts who haunt the mansion.

Bryan Bush, manager of the Perryville Battlefield State Historic Site and an author himself, had plenty of tales of long-dead soldiers still fighting the largest Civil War battle in Kentucky. In fact, ghost sightings are so common it's like a normal day at the office for him.

Barry "Bear" Gaunt, who greets visitors like old friends, preserves the legacy of Octagon Hall in Franklin with stories of Confederate soldiers who sought refuge in this oddly shaped home with its numerous built-in hiding places.

Phillip Seyfrit, curator of the impressive Battle of Richmond Visitors Center, is a human Energizer Bunny. We've long admired his perseverance in keeping history alive—and interesting. He enthralled us with stories for ninety minutes, even though we popped in unannounced just to ask a couple questions.

If we're ever frightened by something big, hairy, and scary in the woods at night, we hope we have Charlie Raymond on speed dial. He created the Kentucky Bigfoot Research Organization to document eyewitness reports in the commonwealth. He also advocates for protecting the Bigfoots' habitat before they become an endangered species.

If you ever have a chance to take a ghost walk led by Patti Starr, book it. We joined her one night in Bardstown, where she captivated our group with eerie stories of hauntings as we walked through Talbott Tavern and Jailer's Inn and then went down to Pioneer Cemetery.

We're lucky to know some nonjudgmental "know-it-alls" who help us out when we're stumped. Heartfelt thanks to the resourceful Eastern Kentucky University Department of Libraries staff, especially research librarians Kevin Jones and Heather Beirne, who answered probing questions about the popularity of "dark tourism" (visiting battlefields, haunted buildings, and crime scenes), witch burning, and other odd occurrences in Kentucky.

Another unsung hero is Michelle Yates with the Casey County Library, who uncovered the fate of the three Liberty women allegedly abducted by aliens in 1976 by tracking down their distant relatives. You have to love small towns and the tenacity of librarians who don't give up. That chapter was inspired, in part, by Elizabeth Orndorff's play *High Strangeness*, which we saw at Danville's Pioneer Playhouse. Elizabeth responded quickly to our email concerning her research into that traumatic incident, which provided valuable insights for this book.

Jeff Moreland, of the *Advocate-Messenger* in Danville, also offered his professional help and support.

As part of the Humanities Council's Speakers Bureau, we have spoken at public libraries and other venues across Kentucky about these paranormal accounts. We appreciate the bookings in Winchester, Stanford, Georgetown, Hodgenville, Bedford, Greenville, Burkesville, Dry Ridge, Shelbyville, Hartford, Erlanger, Somerset, and other locales and the opportunity to marvel over the incredible facilities and programs offered there.

A highlight of our writing career has been collaborating with Hal Blythe and Charlie Sweet, retired English professors at Eastern Kentucky University, and with the late Richard Givan on a ten-book Kentucky-based series, written in just six years, under the name Quinn MacHollister. Their creativity and devious plot ideas amazed, inspired, and sometimes scared us. And, as you might suspect, Bigfoots, werewolves, and a few aliens worked their way into the novels set in the fictional Clement County, Kentucky.

Finally, we'd be remiss (and apologizing forever) if we didn't thank the family members who have humored our "healthy" interest in the paranormal. They've tolerated Bigfoot and alien paraphernalia on display at our home, on the sweatshirts we wear, and featured at the conventions we attend.

Whether you're a believer or a skeptic, we'll leave you with a story about how the topic of paranormal encounters can be a guaranteed conversation starter: One evening, our oldest daughter and her soccer team were celebrating a win at a favorite restaurant. The girls sat at one table, the fathers at another. The dads came from different backgrounds and had varied interests, so they tried to connect with college sports chatter and discussions of local happenings and school events. These topics were quickly exhausted, followed by an awkward silence. Then Mason mentioned a fun fact he'd heard on *Finding Bigfoot*. Suddenly, every dad had something to say. They became animated, excited, engaged—and bonded for life. They all had an opinion about Bigfoot. And they all knew a guy who knew a guy whose brother-in-law saw one of those huge things in the woods back in the day.

So, one sure way to liven up a party is to embrace the weird in Kentucky. Be a name dropper: names like Bigfoot, Goatman, or little green men. Get outdoors, take a hike, stay alert, and be prepared for anything. Like the *Finding Bigfoot* team, you might hear a Squatch in the woods. Or you might find a ghost in your closet or spot a monster in the lake. We guarantee it will make for interesting dinner conversation.

NOTES

INTRODUCTION

1. Troy Taylor, "Waverly Hills Sanitorium: Kentucky Hospital of the Damned," American Hauntings, https://www.americanhauntingsink.com/waverlytb (accessed March 9, 2024).

KENTUCKIANS BATTLE WARTIME FEAR

1. Col. John G. Murphy, "Activities of the Ninth Army AAA—L.A. 'Attacked,'" *Antiaircraft Journal, United States Coast Artillery Association* 82, no. 3 (1949): 5.

2. Stanton T. Friedman, *Flying Saucers and Science: A Scientist Investigates the Mysteries of UFOs* (New York: New Page Books, 2008).

3. Carl Sagan, *The Demon-Haunted World: Science as a Candle in the Dark* (New York: Ballantine, 2011).

4. Don Everitt, *K-Boats: Steam-Powered Submarines in World War I* (Annapolis, MD: Naval Institute Press, 1999), 10.

"I'M CLOSING ON IT"

1. "P-51 Blows up Killing Hero over Franklin," *Louisville Courier-Journal*, January 8, 1948, A1+, Proquest.com newspaper database.

2. Kevin D. Randle, *The UFO Casebook* (New York: Time-Warner Books, 1989), 19–27.

3. Jerome Clark, *The UFO Book: Encyclopedia of the Extraterrestrial* (Detroit: Visible Ink Press, 1997), 351–56.

4. Edward J. Ruppelt, *The Report on Unidentified Flying Objects* [1956] (Nampa, ID: Pacific Publishing, 2011), 19.

5. Donald Keyhoe, *The Flying Saucers Are Real* (New York: Gold Medal Books, 1950), 8.

6. Randle, *UFO Casebook*, 23.

7. Ruppelt, *Report*, 23.

8. Richard Dolan, *UFOs for the 21st Century Mind* (n.p.: Richard Dolan Press, 2014), 128.

9. Ruppelt, *Report*, 23.

10. Ruppelt, Report, 24.

11. John G. Magee Jr., "High Flight" (1941), National Poetry Day, https://nationalpoetryday.co.uk/poem/high-flight/ (accessed March 28, 2022).

12. Dorothy (D. C.) Fontana, "Tomorrow Is Yesterday," *Star Trek: The Original Series*, produced by Gene Roddenberry, Desilu/Paramount, aired January 26, 1967.

13. Randle, *UFO Casebook*, 27.

ALIEN ATTACK

1. Edward J. Ruppelt, *The Report on Unidentified Flying Objects* [1956] (Nampa, ID: Pacific Publishing, 2011).

2. J. T. Gooch, "The Little Green Men of Kelly," in *The Pennyrile: History, Stories, Legends* (n.p.: Whippoorwill Press, 1982).

3. Daniel Cohen, *Encyclopedia of Monsters* (New York: Dodd Mead, 1987).

4. Tim Ghianni, "Did Aliens Land Here? Fifty Years Later, the People of Kelly, Ky., Are Still Debating That," *Tennessean Sunday Magazine*, August 7, 2005, 50–56.

5. Geraldine Sutton Stith, *Alien Legacy: Based on a True Event* (n.p.: Author House, 2007).

6. Stith, *Alien Legacy*, 37.

7. Ghianni, "Did Aliens Land Here?" 52.

8. Stith, *Alien Legacy*.

9. Adam May, email message to the authors, March 22, 2022.

10. Michele Carlton, "Kelly Green Men," *Kentucky New Era*, December 30, 2002, https://www.kentuckynewera.com/article_d231aaad-127a-51b1-84a3-db58416e2425.html.

11. Stith, *Alien Legacy*, xxx.

12. Joe Nickell, "Attack of the Little Green Men," in *Tracking the Man Beasts: Sasquatch, Vampires, Zombies, and More* (Amherst, NY: Prometheus Books, 2011), 167–73.

13. Nickell, "Attack of the Little Green Men," 172.

14. J. Allen Hynek, *The Hynek UFO Report* (1977; reprint, Newburyport, MA: Red Wheel/Weiser Books, 2020), 209.

15. Gooch, "Little Green Men of Kelly."

16. Leslie Kean, *UFOs: Generals, Pilots, and Government Officials Go on the Record* (New York: Three Rivers Press, 2010), 284.

17. Nick Pope, *Open Skies, Closed Minds: For the First Time a Government UFO Expert Speaks Out* (New York: Dell, 1998).

18. David Talbot, *The Devil's Chessboard: Allen Dulles, the CIA, and the Rise of America's Secret Government* (New York: Harpers, 2015).

THE LONG ROAD HOME

1. Emma Austin, "A Shootout, a Fatal Chase, and Alien Abductions: 5 Times Kentuckians Say They Saw a UFO," *Louisville Courier-Journal*, June 22, 2021, https://www.courier-journal.com/story/news/history/2021/06/22/kentucky-ufo-sightings-5-times-aliens-reported-in-bluegrass-state/7076190002/.

2. Jerome Clark, *The UFO Book* (Canton, MI: Visible Ink Press, 1998), 319.

3. Larry Rowell, "Casey Women's 1976 Experience Basis for Play," *Casey County News*, September 26, 2010.

4. Christopher Kemp, "Close Encounter with Jerry Black: There's Something out There ... UFO Sighting in Central Kentucky," *Ace Weekly*, January 3, 2022, https://www.aceweekly.com/BackissuesACEWeekly/010322/cover_story010322.html.

5. John Greenewald, "The 1976 Stanford, Kentucky, Abductions," theblackvault.com, April 26, 2016, https://www.theblackvault.com/casefiles/1976-stanford-kentucky-abductions/.

6. B. J. Booth, "Stanford Incident," Whatsupwithufos.com, https://whatsupwithufos.com/Three_Kentucky_Women_Claimed_to_Have_Been_Abducted_While_Driving_at_Night/ (accessed March 22, 2022).

7. Clark, *UFO Book*, 320.

8. "The Stanford Abduction," Kentuckyfandom.com, https://Completely-Kentucky.fandom.com/wiki/Stanford_Abduction (accessed March 21, 2022).

9. Clark, *UFO Book*, 321.

10. Greenewald, "1976 Stanford, Kentucky, Abductions."

11. Brenda Edwards, "Possible UFOs? Strange Objects Seen in Sky in Lincoln County," *Kentucky Advocate*, February 1, 1976, 28.

12. Coleman Larkin, "15 Times Aliens Definitely Visited Kentucky," Kyforky.com, September 19, 2019, https://kyforky.com/blogs/journal/15-times-aliens-definitely-visited-kentucky.

13. Kemp, "Close Encounter with Jerry Black."

14. Booth, "Stanford Incident."

15. Booth, "Stanford Incident."

16. "Kentucky Abductions," *APRO Bulletin* 25, no. 4 (October 1976): 6, cited in Charles Lear, "A 1976 UFO Encounter in Kentucky," Podcast UFO Live, January 30, 2022, https://podcastufo.com/a-1976-ufo-encounter-in-kentucky/#more-2711.

17. Rowell, "Casey Women's 1976 Experience."

18. Booth, "Stanford Incident."

19. Kemp, "Close Encounter with Jerry Black."

20. Booth, "Stanford Incident."

21. Gemma Pastor Cerezuela et al., "Wertheim's Hypothesis on 'Highway Hypnosis': Empirical Evidence from a Study on Motorway and Conventional Road Driving," *Accident Analysis and Prevention* 36, no. 6 (2004): 1045–54.

22. Shahram Rafieian and Steven Hosier, "Dissociative Experiences in Health and Disease," *Human Architecture: Journal of the Sociology of Self-Knowledge* 9, no. 1 (2011): 89–109.

23. "Kentucky Abductions."

24. John A. Keel, *The Mothman Prophecies* (New York: Tor Books, 1975).

25. Elaine Thomas obituary, *Danville Advocate-Messenger*, September 26, 1978.

26. Louise Smith obituary, *Danville Advocate-Messenger*, August 24, 2003.

27. Rowell, "Casey Women's 1976 Experience."

ALL ABOARD!

1. "Paintsville UFO and Train Collision," Completely Kentucky Wiki, https://completely-kentucky.fandom.com/wiki/Paintsville_UFO_and_Train_Collision (accessed June 14, 2022).

2. Joey Balto, "Train Hits UFO, Paintsville, KY," Trainorders.com, July 2006, https://www.trainorders.com/discussion/read.php?2,1205108.

3. "January 2002 Weather History in Louisville, Kentucky," Weatherspark.com, https://weatherspark.com/h/m/15227/2002/1/Historical-Weather-in-January-2002-in-Louisville-Kentucky-United-States.

4. Tim Preston, "UFO Sightings Abundant in Eastern Kentucky; MUFON Investigating," *Ashland Daily Independent*, February 16, 2011, https://www.dailyindependent.com/news/local_news/ufo-sightings-abundant-in-eastern-kentucky-mufon-investigating/article_862d8547-a7dc-5d36-848a-f1e68e0f281e.html.

5. "How Many Passengers Are Flying Right Now?" Spike Aerospace, https://www.spikeaerospace.com/how-many-passengers-are-flying-right-now/ (accessed June 14, 2022).

6. Scott Sutherland, "Stunning Jellyfish Sprite Seen in the Night Sky during Texas Storm," The Weather Network, August 20, 2020, https://www.theweathernetwork.com/ca/news/article/spectacular-jellyfish-sprite-captured-what-causes-these-strange-events.

7. Kenny Young, "Kentucky UFO Sightings and Screaming Sounds Linked," UFO Casebook, November 20, 2003, https://www.ufocasebook.com/kentuckyufoscreaming.html.

8. Young, "Kentucky UFO Sightings and Screaming Sounds Linked."

9. Christina Nunez, "Ball Lightning: Weird, Mysterious, Perplexing, and Deadly," *National Geographic*, March 5, 2019, https://www.nationalgeographic.com/environment/article/ball-lightning/.

10. "Ball Lightning," *Encyclopedia Britannica*, http://britannica.com/science/ball-lightning (accessed July 20, 2022).

11. Jerome Clark, *The UFO Book* (Canton, MI: Visible Ink Press, 1998), 369.

12. US Department of Defense, "The Department of Defense Releases the President's Fiscal Year 2022 Defense Budget," May 28, 2021, https://www.defense.gov/News/Releases/Release/Article/2638711/the-department-of-defense-releases-the-presidents-fiscal-year-2022-defense-budget/.

13. Robert Beckhusen and Noah Shachtman, "See for Yourself: The Pentagon's $51 Billion 'Black' Budget," *Wired*, February 15, 2012, https://www.wired.com/2012/02/pentagons-black-budget.

14. Alejandro Rojas, "Lockheed Skunk Works Director Says ESP Is the Key to Interstellar Travel," Open Minds: Credible UFO News and Information, July 26, 2013, http://www.openminds.tv/lockheed-skunk-works-director-says-esp-is-the-key-to-interstellar-travel-video-1092/23042.

THE NEVER-ENDING STRUGGLE

1. "Book: 'Perryville: This Grand Havoc of Battle'; An Interview with Historian Ken Noe," American Battlefield Trust, https://www.battlefields.org/learn/articles/book-perryville-grand-havoc-battle (accessed April 8, 2024).

2. Bryan Bush and Thomas Freese, *Haunted Battlefields of the South* (Atglen, PA: Schiffer Books, 2010), 58–59.

3. Bush and Freese, *Haunted Battlefields of the South*, 55.

4. "Haunted Perryville," *Kentucky Life*, KET.org, October 26, 2019, https://www.youtube.com/watch?v=Q18wM7BTcmI.

5. Leslie Kean, *Surviving Death: A Journalist Investigates Evidence of an Afterlife* (New York: Crown Archetype Press, 2017), 230.

6. "Battle of Perryville," American Battlefield Trust, https://www.battlefields.org/learn/civil-war/battles/perryville (accessed June 27, 2022).

7. Andrea Limke, "The Mysterious Kentucky Town That's Home to More Ghosts Than People," Only in Your State, January 12, 2019, https://www.onlyinyourstate.com/kentucky/most-haunted-town-ky/.

8. Colin Dickey, *Ghostland: An American History in Haunted Places* (New York: Penguin, 2017).

SEARCHING FOR WRAITHS IN ALL THE WRONG PLACES

1. "History: Battle of Richmond," https://www.battleofrichmond.com/history (accessed April 15, 2024).

2. R&S Exploring, "Richmond, Kentucky, Civil War Battlefield," YouTube, https://www.youtube.com/watch?v=b6BjiaqmAl0 (accessed April 11, 2024).

3. Madison County, Kentucky, https://madisoncountyky.us/index.php/the-battle-of-richmond (accessed July 30, 2022).

4. Thomas Leonard Livermore, *Numbers and Losses in the Civil War in America, 1861–1865* (Boston: Houghton, Mifflin, 1900), 89–90.

5. "Richmond Battle Facts and Summary," American Battlefield Trust, https://www.battlefields.org/learn/civil-war/battles/richmond (accessed April 9, 2024).

6. William Lynwood Montell, *Haunted Houses and Family Ghosts of Kentucky* (Lexington: University Press of Kentucky, 2001), 219–20.

7. Montell, *Haunted Houses and Family Ghosts of Kentucky*, xiv.

8. Tracy Kidder, *House* (New York: Houghton Mifflin Harcourt, 1999).

9. Spooky2066, "Has Anyone Had Any Ghost Experiences at Civil War Battlefields?" Reddit.com, 2022, https://www.reddit.com/r/Ghoststories/comments/uslegn/has_anyone_had_any_ghost_experiences_at_civil_war/.

10. Alan Brown, *Kentucky Legends and Lore* (Charleston, SC: History Press, 2021), 162.

11. "Camp Nelson National Cemetery/Historical Information," National Cemetery Administration, https://www.cem.va.gov/cems/nchp/campnelson.asp#hi (accessed April 11, 2024).

12. "Camp Nelson," American Battlefield Trust, October 27, 2018, https://www.battlefields.org/news/american-battlefield-trust-praises-designation-camp-nelson-national-monument.

13. Tim Talbott, "First USCT Recruits at Camp Nelson," Explore Kentucky History, https://explorekyhistory.ky.gov/items/show/192 (accessed April 11, 2024).

14. "Hospitals and Medical Facilities," Camp Nelson National Monument, National Park Service, https://www.nps.gov/cane/learn/historyculture/hospitals.htm (accessed April 11, 2024).

15. Marie Mitchell, "Paranormal Is Normal," *Richmond Register*, December 18, 2021, A5.

16. *Saving Private Ryan*, directed by Steven Spielberg (Dreamworks/Paramount/Amblin, 1998), https://www.youtube.com/watch?v=IZgoufN99n8.

CIVIL WAR CASUALTIES

1. Interview with Barry "Bear" Gaunt, Octagon Hall, Franklin, Kentucky, July 15, 2022.

2. Jackie Hollenkamp Bentley, "Spirited Site," *Kentucky Monthly*, September 30, 2021, http://www.kentuckymonthly.com/explore/places/a-spirited-site/.

3. Sarah Denson, "Is Octagon Hall the Most Haunted House in the South?" WKRN, Nashville, October 26, 2017, updated October 1, 2019, https://www.wkrn.com/?submit=&s=Octagon+Hall.

4. Bentley, "Spirited Site."

5. Bentley, "Spirited Site."

6. Denson, "Is Octagon Hall Most Haunted?"

7. Denson, "Is Octagon Hall Most Haunted?"

8. Shannon Sinn, "The Indigenous Burial Ground: Urban Legends and Popular Culture," Folklore Thursday, March 3, 2022, https://folklorethursday.com/regional-folklore/indigenous-burial-ground.

9. Colin Dickey, *Ghostland: An American History in Haunted Places* (New York: Penguin, 2016), 215.

10. "The Ley of the Land," *Guardian*, May 12, 2000, https://www.theguardian.com/theguardian/2000/may/13/weekend7.weekend1.

11. Hannah Osborne, "Skinwalker Ranch: The UFO Hotspot in Utah That Has Men Obsessed," *Newsweek*, April 28, 2022, https://www.newsweek.com/ufo-skinwalker-ranch-utah-pentagon-paranormal-1701730.

12. "Groundwater Resources in Kentucky," http://www.uky.edu/KGS/water/library/gwatlas/Simpson/Waterquality.htm (accessed August 11, 2022).

13. Lynne Hume, *Portals: Opening Doorways to Other Realities through the Senses* (New York: Routledge Taylor & Francis Group, 2007), 15.

14. Dickey, *Ghostland*, 77.

MARY TODD LINCOLN SEEKS SOLACE IN SÉANCES

1. Alexandra Kommel, "Seances in the Red Room: How Spiritualism Comforted the Nation during and after the Civil War," White House Historical Association, April 24, 2019, https://www.whitehousehistory.org/seances-in-the-red-room.

2. "Biography: Mary Todd Lincoln," Mary Todd Lincoln House, https://www.mtlhouse.org/biography (accessed August 9, 2022).

3. "Biography: Mary Todd Lincoln."

4. "Residents and Visitors: Mary's Charlatans," Mr. Lincoln's White House, Gilder Lehrman Institute of American History, https://www.mrlincolnswhitehouse.org/residents-visitors/marys-charlatans/ (accessed August 11, 2022).

5. "Biography: Mary Todd Lincoln."

6. "Residents and Visitors."

7. "Residents and Visitors."

8. Terry Alford, "The Spiritualist Who Warned Lincoln Was Also Booth's Drinking Buddy," *Smithsonian*, March 2015, https://www.smithsonianmag.com/history/the-spiritualist-who-warned-lincoln-was-also-booths-drinking-buddy-180954317/.

9. Alford, "Spiritualist Who Warned Lincoln."

10. "Residents and Visitors."

11. Alford, "Spiritualist Who Warned Lincoln."

12. "Residents and Visitors."

13. Alford, "Spiritualist Who Warned Lincoln."

14. Roger J. Norton, "Mary Todd Lincoln and Clairvoyance," Rogerjnorton.com (accessed July 20, 2022).

15. Alford, "Spiritualist Who Warned Lincoln."

16. Mitch Horowitz, "Mary Todd Lincoln: Spiritualist," July 16, 2018, www.medium.com.

17. Jesse Gormley, "The Lincolns Brought Spiritualism and Seances to the White House," Ripley's, June 26, 2021, www.ripleys.com.

18. Alford, "Spiritualist Who Warned Lincoln."

19. Kaleena Fraga and Leah Silverman, "Mary Todd Lincoln: American History's Most Misunderstood First Lady," All That's Interesting, December 16, 2021, https://allthatsinteresting.com/mary-todd-lincoln.

20. Norton, "Mary Todd Lincoln and Clairvoyance."

21. Jordan Lilies, "Did Abraham Lincoln's Ghost Appear in an 1872 Photo?" Snopes.com, February 3, 2021, https://www.snopes.com/fact-check/abraham-lincoln-ghost-photo/.

THE HAND ON THE RAILING

1. Kevin McQueen, *Cassius M. Clay: Freedom's Champion* (Paducah, KY: Turner Publishing, 2001), 73–93.

2. Michael Medved, "Americans Should Know the Story of Abolitionist Cassius Clay: Muhammad Ali's Namesake Risked His Career, Wealth, and Life to Promote Emancipation," *Wall Street Journal*, June 21, 2021, https://www.wsj.com/articles/americans-should-know-the-story-of-abolitionist-cassius-clay-11624053172.

3. Quoted in Medved, "Americans Should Know."

4. White Hall State Historic Site, https://whitehall.eku.edu/ (accessed May 23, 2022).

5. Grant Wilson, Speech to Model Laboratory School, Richmond, KY, February 12, 2016.

6. John Blake, "Ghost Hunters Say This Is Their Biggest Fear. And It Has Nothing to Do with Ghosts," CNN, October 26, 2019, https://www.cnn.com/2019/10/26/us/ghost-hunters-paranormal-blake/index.htm.

7. McQueen, *Cassius M. Clay*, 81.

8. Colin Dickey, *Ghostland: An American History in Haunted Places* (New York: Penguin, 2017), 284.

9. Dickey, *Ghostland*, 48.

10. Colin Dickey, *The Unidentified: Mythical Monsters, Alien Encounters, and Our Obsession with the Unexplained* (New York: Viking, 2020).

THE GRAY LADY

1. "The Brown Lady–1936," The Most Famous Ghost Photographs Ever Taken, https://www.pocket-lint.com/cameras/news/141224-the-most-famous-ghost-photographs-ever-taken (accessed August 3, 2022).

2. "Learn: The Brown Family," Liberty Hall Historic Site, Libertyhall.org (accessed August 3, 2022).

3. "Visit: About Frankfort: City History," http://www.Frankfort.ky.gov (accessed August 3, 2022).

4. "Learn: The Brown Family."

5. Susan L. Moore, "'Our Beloved Ghost' of Liberty Hall," *Frank*, October 1, 2019, https://frankthemagazine.com/our-beloved-ghost-of-liberty-hall/.

6. Moore, "'Our Beloved Ghost.'"

7. "Learn: The Brown Family."

8. "Learn: The Brown Family."

9. Moore, "'Our Beloved Ghost.'"

10. Moore, "'Our Beloved Ghost.'"

11. "Learn: The Brown Family."

12. Moore, "'Our Beloved Ghost.'"

13. Hans Holzer, *Ghosts: True Encounters with the World Beyond* (1968; reprint, New York: Black Dog & Leventhal, 2012), 145.

14. Mary Chase, *Harvey: A Comedy in Three Acts* (New York: Snowball Publishing, 1971; reprint, 2014).

STILL HANGING AROUND

1. "Biography: Jesse James," *The American Experience*, PBS, https://www.pbs.org/wgbh/americanexperience/features/james-jesse/ (accessed August 8, 2022).

2. Jenn Shockley, "The Top Eight Most Haunted Places in Kentucky," Kentucky for Kentucky, October 26, 2016, https://kyforky.com/blogs/journal/haunted-places?_pos=2&_sid=ac5347ca6&_ss=r.

3. "Ghost Encounters at the Tavern," Talbott Tavern, https://talbotttavern.com/ghost-encounters/ (accessed August 7, 2022).

4. Todd Atteberry, "America's Haunted Inns: Bardstown Kentucky's Chilling Old Talbott Tavern Lives up to Its Reputation," http://gothichorrorstories.com (accessed August 7, 2022).

5. Jim Larkin, "Country Kitchens," *Travel and Leisure*, June 2003, http://travelandleisure.com/country_kitchens/june_2003.

6. Atteberry, "America's Haunted Inns."

7. "Study Reveals Secrets behind Ghost Tour Boom," Goldsmith College, University of London, www.gold.ac.uk (accessed August 2, 2022), citing Gavin Weston, Justin Woodman, Helen Cornish, and Natalie Djohari, "Spectral Cities: Death and Living Memories in the Dark Tourism of British Ghost Walks," *Urbanities: A Journal of Urban Ethology* (November 2019).

8. Todd Atteberry, "Author: A Gothic Curiosity," https://www.gothichorrorstories.com/bio/about-a-gothic-cabinet-of-curiosity-and-mysteries/ (accessed August 8, 2022).

DARK TOURISM

1. Hannah Sampson, "Dark Tourism, Explained: Why Tourists Flock to Sites of Tragedy," *Washington Post*, November 13, 2019, https://www.washingtonpost.com/graphics/2019/travel/dark-tourism-explainer/.

2. Jeff Waldridge and John Cosper, *The Haunting of a Bourbon Town* (Monroe, IL: Dead Park Books, 2023).

3. "Plasma Balls for Ghost Hunting," Reddit, https://www.reddit.com/r/GhostHunting/comments/169t5j3/plasma_balls_for_ghost_hunting/ (accessed April 6, 2024).

4. John Zaffis and Brian McLityre, *Shadows in the Dark* (Lincoln, NE: iUniverse, 2004), 39.

5. Aja Romero, "From Amityville to Annabelle, the Warrens on Film Are a Lie," Vox, October 21, 2023, https://www.vox.com/culture/23939024/ed-lorraine-warren-cases-hoax-real-conjuring-amityville.

6. "Unmatched History," Buffalo Trace Distillery, 2022, https://www.buffalotracedistillery.com/unmatched-history.html.

7. Brent Owen, "Spirited Tales," *Kentucky Monthly*, October 1, 2017, http://www.kentuckymonthly.com/culture/history/spirited-tales/.

8. Liz Carey, "Road Culture: At Kentucky's Oldest Distilleries, Spirits Fill the Bourbon Barrels, and Haunt the Halls," Roadtrippers.com, October 20, 2019, https://roadtrippers.com/magazine/kentucky-haunted-distilleries.

THE SEARCH FOR APPALACHIAN GHOSTS

1. Diligent-Ice1276, "Is It True That the Appalachian Mountains Are Haunted?" Reddit.com, https://www.reddit.com/r/Appalachia/comments/16iep9m/is_it_true_that_the_appalachian_mountains_are/ (accessed April 12, 2024).

2. R. Zackery Youngblood, "Southern Appalachian Ghost Stories," academic paper for Introduction to Folklore, Brigham Young University, April 16, 2022, https://contentdm.lib.byu.edu/digital/api/collection/folklore/id/1663/download.

3. Raven Willow, "The Ghost Bride of Cumberland Falls," https://vocal.media/horror/the-ghost-bride (accessed March 8, 2024).

4. Spicy-Pickled-Okra, "Is It True That the Appalachian Mountains Are Haunted?" Reddit.com.

5. Patrick W. Gainer, introduction to *Witches, Ghosts, and Signs: Folklore of the Southern Appalachians* (Morgantown, WV: Vandalia Press, 2008), xxii.

6. Leonard W. Roberts, *South of Hell-fer-Sartin: Kentucky Mountain Folk Tales* (Lexington: University Press of Kentucky, 1988).

7. Bill Ellis, *Aliens, Ghosts, and Cults: Legends We Live* (Jackson: University Press of Mississippi, 2003), 11.

8. Cassandra Yorgey, "Appalachia's Many Abandoned Coal Mines Are Rumored to Be Haunted: Some Still Hear the Axes of the Miners Echoing in Tunnels," *Extempore News*, February 2, 2023, http://extempore.com/news/appalachia-haunted-coal-mines.

9. Cal Winslow, "A Brief History of Harlan County, USA," Labor Notes, August 2019, https://labornotes.org/blogs/2019/08/brief-history-harlan-county-usa.

10. Steve Gilly and Rod Mullins, "Headless Annie," Mountain Lore: Tales from Appalachia, May 4, 2018, https://mountainlore.net/2018/05/04/headless-annie/.

11. Garrett Shaw, "Visiting the Highest Point in Kentucky," YouTube, https://www.youtube.com/watch?v=oksW02mIgVM (accessed March 9, 2024).

THE TRAGIC TALE OF THE BATTLETOWN WITCH

1. "The Battletown Witch," Weird Meade County, www.weirdmeadecounty.com/thebattletown-witch (accessed September 16, 2022).

2. Evan Andrews, "Were Witches Burned at the Stake during the Salem Witch Trials?" History.com, September 1, 2018, https://www.history.com/news/were-witches-burned-at-the-stake-during-the-salem-witchtrials#:~:text=Twenty%20people%20were%20eventually%20executed,Hill%20to%20die%20by%20hanging.

3. Gerald W. Fischer, *Battletown Witch: Leah Smock, the Evolution of Witchcraft, and the Last Witch Burning in America* (Morley, MO: Acclaim Press, 2016), 91.

4. Charlie Hicks, "Halloween Tales of Meade County Haunts," *Meade County Messenger*, October 27, 1977, 1.

5. Kay Hamilton, *Burned as a Witch: The Legend of Leah Smock* (Brandenburg, KY: Bearhead Publishing, 2016).

6. "Leah Smock the Witch of Battletown, Ky.," Unknown Kentucky, March 21, 2014, https://www.facebook.com/681025945276661/photos/leah-smock-the-witch-of-battletown-kyleah-smock-was-born-in-1818-near-battletown/693640450681877/.

7. Fischer, *Battletown Witch*, 132.

8. Fischer, *Battletown Witch*, 91.

9. Fischer, *Battletown Witch*, 141.

10. Fischer, *Battletown Witch*, 20.

11. "The Power of the Placebo Effect," *Harvard Health*, December 13, 2021, https://www.health.harvard.edu/mental-health/the-power-of-the-placebo-effect.

12. Translation from Proz.com, https://www.proz.com/kudoz/spanish-to-english/idioms-maxims-sayings/1308413-las-brujas-no-existen-pero-que-las-hay-las-hay.html (accessed October 17, 2022).

BIGFOOT BOOGIE

1. "State Listings: Kentucky," Bigfoot Field Research Organization (BFRO), https://www.bfro.net/GDB/state_listing.asp?state=ky (accessed March 25, 2024).

2. Charlie Raymond, "Reports," Kentucky Bigfoot Research Organization (KBRO), http://kentuckybigfoot.com (accessed June 20, 2020).

3. Marie Mitchell, "Tales of Bigfoot in Kentucky," *Richmond Register*, November 23, 2011, https://www.richmondregister.com/news/lifestyles/tales-of-bigfoot-in-kentucky/article_e790b60f-8a20-56f2-989b-28586c6776a9.html.

4. Barton Nunnelly, *Mysterious Kentucky*, vol. 1, *The History, Mystery and Unexplained of the Bluegrass State* (n.p.: Triangulum Publishing, 2017), 108.

5. Barton M. Nunnelly, *Bigfoot in Kentucky: On the Trail of Giants in the Bluegrass State* (Chicago: Whitechapel Press, 2011), 55–56.

6. "Reports," KBRO, https://www.kentuckybigfoot.com/reports.htm (accessed September 5, 2022).

7. Nunnelly, *Mysterious Kentucky*.

8. "Wildman Days," Facebook, http://facebook.com/wildmandaysKY/ (accessed April 12, 2024).

9. Frank Boyett, "Spottsville Monster Comes to Life on TV: Show Recalls Family's 1975 Encounter," *Henderson Gleaner*, March 18, 2015, https://www.newspapers.com/image/771881620.

10. Nunnelly, *Mysterious Kentucky*, 158.

11. Nunnelly, *Bigfoot in Kentucky*, 55.

12. Charlie Raymond, KBRO website, https://www.kentuckybigfoot.com/QandA.htm (accessed September 5, 2022).

13. FAQ: "Are They Dangerous?" BFRO, https://www.bfro.net/gdb/show_FAQ.asp?id=659 (accessed June 23, 2022).

14. Ben Tobin, "Bigfoot Sighting in Kentucky? Couple Recounts Bizarre Tale at Mammoth Cave," *Louisville Courier-Journal*, July 31, 2019, https://www.courier-journal.com/story/news/local/2019/07/31/man-mammoth-cave-fires-shot-over-alleged-bigfoot-sighting-report/1875745001/.

15. Nunnelly, *Bigfoot in Kentucky*, 56.

16. FAQ: "Behavior," BFRO.

17. Liz Langley, "You Can't Kill Bigfoot in Washington, and More Odd Animal Laws," *National Geographic*, August 31, 2017, https://ww.nationalgeographic.com/animals/article/weird-laws-nation-dogs-ferrets-bigfoot.

18. "Species Information," Kentucky Department of Fish and Wildlife, https://app.fw.ky.gov/speciesinfo/speciesList.asp?strGroup=1&strSort1=Class&strSort2=CommonName (accessed March 27, 2024).

VICIOUS MAN-WOLF STALKS LAND BETWEEN THE LAKES

1. "Land Between the Lakes National Recreation Area," US Forest Service, US Department of Agriculture, www.landbetweenthelakes.us/about/ (accessed January 26, 2022).

2. "Officials Confirm that Animal Killed by Ky. Hunter in March Was Endangered Gray Wolf," Timber Wolf Information Network, March 2024, https://www.timberwolfinformation.org/ky-officials-confirm-that-animal-killed-by-ky-hunter-in-march-was-endangered-gray-wolf/.

3. Ron Coffey, *Kentucky Cryptids: "Monsters" from the Bluegrass State* (Somerville, MA: Fairy Ring Press, 2018), 61.

4. "Wildlife Species," Kentucky Department of Fish and Wildlife, www.fw.ky.gov/Pages/Wildlife-Species.aspx (accessed March 5, 2022).

5. Coffey, *Kentucky Cryptids*, 65.

6. *American Werewolves*, directed by Seth Breedlove (Small Town Monsters, 2022).

7. Martha C. Sims and Martine Stephens, *Living Folklore: Introduction to the Study of People and Their Traditions* (Logan: Utah State University Press, 2005).

8. Linda S. Godfrey, *Real Wolfmen: True Encounters in Modern America* (New York: Jeremey P. Tarcher/Penguin, 2012), 231–54, 278.

9. "Racial Memory," in *The APA Dictionary of Psychology*, https://dictionary.apa.org/racial-memory (accessed February 22, 2022).

10. Nora Sayer, *Running Time: Films of the Cold War* (New York: Dial Press, 1982).

11. Jim Wayne Miller, "After Twenty Years," *Ashville Poetry Review* 2, no. 1 (1995), http://www.ashevillepoetryreview.com/1995/issue-3/after-twenty-years.

DEVIOUS GOATMAN LURES VICTIMS ONTO COAL TRAIN TRESTLE

1. Sarah Ladd, "Girl Dies, Another Injured in Latest Tragedy on Trestle," *Louisville Courier-Journal*, May 29, 2019, A3, https://www.newspapers.com/image/568902826/?terms=%22Pope%20Lick%20trestle%22&match=1.

2. Ladd, "Girl Dies, Another Injured," A3.

3. Ben Guarino, "Couple's Curiosity About Kentucky's 'Goatman' Legend Takes Fatal Turn on Railroad Trestle," *Washington Post*, April 26, 2016, http://www.washingtonpost.com.

4. Richard Stottman, "Legends of the Deadly Pope Lick Trestle: Deaths & Injuries from Real Monsters," Beargrassthunder.com, posted October 13, 2021, updated October 20, 2021, https://www.beargrassthunder.com/post/legend-of-the-pope-lick-trestle.

5. Beth Warren, "Pope Lick Monster Mythical, Dangers Real," *Louisville Courier-Journal*, May 14, 2016, www.courier-journal.com/story/news/local/2016/05/14/pop.

6. "Legend at Pope Lick Immersive Horror Escape," 30-Minute Outdoor Immersive Horror Experience, https://mostfunyoueverhad.resova.us/ (accessed October 25, 2022).

7. "Searching for the Pope Lick Monster," Video Zone, https://www.youtube.com/watch?v=Hx0QZqs5v34 (accessed April 29, 2022).

8. Steve Rush, "The Monster at Pope Lick," *New Voice*, October 21, 1990, 1A.

9. Dawn Gee, "The Legend of the Goatman," WAVE 3 News, May 10, 2014, updated June 24, 2014, https://m.facebook.com/wave3news/posts/10152355966893686.

10. Wesley Carter, narrator, "The Goatman Monster of Pope Lick," SpooKY Stories, Beargrass Thunder, https://www.youtube.com/watch?v=5LJ6-LNI9Bc (accessed April 29, 2022).

11. "The Pope Lick Monster," WDRB.com, October 13, 2013.

12. Stottman, "Legends of the Deadly Pope Lick Trestle."

13. Stottman, "Legends of the Deadly Pope Lick Trestle."

14. Judy Bryant and Lisa Jessie, "Film Puts Pope Lick Trestle's Fatal Attraction in the Spotlight," *Louisville Courier-Journal*, January 5, 1989, https://www.newspapers.com/image/110593208/?terms=Pope%20Lick&match=1.

15. "Pope Lick Monster," WDRB.com.

16. Mary Ellen Brown and Bruce A. Rosenberg, eds., "Trolls," in *Encyclopedia of Folklore and Literature* (ABC-CLIO eBook, 1998), https://legacy-abc-clio-com.libproxy.eku.edu/reader.aspx?isbn=9781576075036&id=FLKLT.703&sidebar=about#.

17. Rich Newman, *Haunted Bridges: Over 300 of America's Creepiest Crossings* (Woodbury, MN: Llewellyn Publications, 2016), 2.

WATER MONSTERS

1. "Lake Herrington Monster," Cryptid Wiki, https://cryptidz.fandom.com/wiki/Lake_Herrington_Monster (accessed June 13, 2022).

2. Joe Ward, "Herrington Lake 'Monster' Reported by Professor," *Louisville Courier-Journal*, August 7, 1972, B1.

3. Art Lander, "Art Lander's Outdoors: Built Nearly a Century Ago, Herrington Lake Is Kentucky's Oldest Major Reservoir," *Northern Kentucky Tribune*, May 14, 2021, https://www.nkytribune.com/2021/05/art-landers-outdoors-built-nearly-a-century-ago-herrington-lake-is-kentuckys-oldest-major-reservoir/.

4. "Herrington Monster" thread, "Kentucky Reports" forum, fishin.com, http://www.fishin.com/forums2/showthread.php/60894-Herrington-Monster?highlight=Lake+Herrington (accessed June 24, 2022).

5. "Herrington Lake Monster," Kentucky Unknown Facebook Group, August 4, 2014, facebook.com/page/681025945276661/search/?q=Lake%20Herrington%20monstger.

6. "Retired UK Library Chief Lawrence Thompson Dies," *Louisville Courier-Journal*, April 21, 1986, A12.

7. Lawrence S. Thompson, "Herrington Lake Monster," letter to the editor, *Lexington Herald*, July 29, 1972, A4.

8. Ward, "Herrington Lake 'Monster,'" B1.

9. George Dudding, *Kentucky's Herrington Lake Monster* (GDParanormal, 2015), 1.

10. "State Record Fishes and Awards," Kentucky Department of Fish and Wildlife, https://fw.ky.gov/Fish/Pages/State-Record-Fishes-and-Awards.aspx (accessed June 9, 2022).

11. Benjamin Radford and Joe Nickell, *Lake Monster Mysteries: Investigating the World's Most Elusive Creatures* (Lexington: University Press of Kentucky, 2006), 1.

MOTHMAN AND DEMON LEAPER SWOOP AROUND KENTUCKY

1. "'Flying Creature' Said Seen along Ohio River," *Lexington Leader*, November 18, 1966, A1, https://www.newspapers.com/image/681055953/?terms=%22Flying%20creature%22&match=1.

2. Erica Bivens, "Mothman Documentary Shot in Kentucky to Debut Next Week," WTVQ-TV, October 16, 2020, https://www.wtvq.com/mothman-documentary-shot-in-kentucky-to-debut-next-week/.

3. "Mothman in Kentucky," *Unusual Kentucky*, June 22, 2008, https://unusualkentucky.blogspot.com/2008/06/mothman-sighting-in-russell.html.

4. Stephanie Hanson, comment on "The Kentucky Mothman," Kentucky Unknown Facebook post, May 7, 2019, https://www.facebook.com/search/top/?q=Kentucky%20Unknown%20.

5. "Mothman," *Monster Quest*, season 4, episode 5, History Channel, air date February 10, 2010.

6. David Domine, *Haunts of Old Louisville* (Kuttawa, KY: McClanahan Publishing, 2009), 66.

7. Domine, *Haunts*, 66.

8. Dawne Gee, "Tales of Kentucky's Gargoyle-like Creature Documented in Headlines," WAVE-TV, May 13, 2014, https://www.wave3.com/story/25507268/demon-leaper/.

9. "An Aerial Mystery," *New York Times*, September 12, 1880, A6, https://www.newspapers.com/clip/68484626/an-aerial-mystery-new-york/.

10. Domine, *Haunts*, 68.

CONCLUSION

1. Augustine, *The City of God*, ed. Etienne Gilson (New York: Doubleday, 1958).

2. Michael Grosso, "Miracles: Illusions, Natural Events, or Divine Interventions?" *Journal of Religious & Psychical Research* 20, no. 4 (October 1997): 182–98, included in Michael Grosso, *Smile of the Universe: Miracles in an Age of Disbelief* (Charlottesville, VA: Anomalist Books, 2020).

3. Mizra Newton, "Scientists Find a Multidimensional Universe Inside the Human Brain," physics-astronomy.com, February 7, 2022.

4. Jerome Clark, introduction to *The UFO Book: Encyclopedia of the Extraterrestrial* (Detroit: Visible Ink Press, 1997), xvi.

5. *2001: A Space Odyssey*, directed by Stanley Kubrick (Warner Bros., 1968).

6. Carl Sagan, *Contact* (New York: Simon and Schuster, 1985), 370.